THE HEART OF THE MAKER

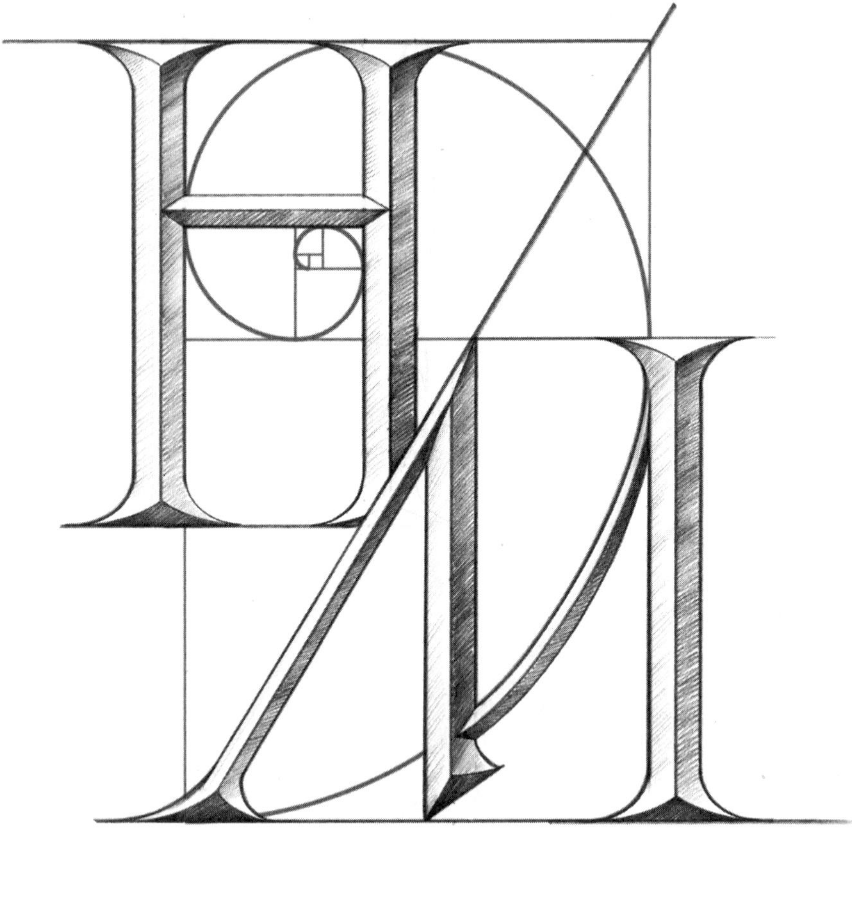

THE HEART OF THE MAKER

HOW TO PUT YOUR PASSION TO WORK

JAKE WEIDMANN

W Publishing Group
An Imprint of Thomas Nelson

The Heart of the Maker

Published by W Publishing, an imprint of Thomas Nelson, 501 Nelson Place, Nashville, TN 37214, USA.

Author is represented by Jenni Burke of Illuminate Literary Agency, www.illluminateliterary.com.

Thomas Nelson titles may be purchased in bulk for educational, business, fundraising, or sales promotional use. For information, please email SpecialMarkets@ThomasNelson.com.

ISBN 978-1-4003-3952-5 (audiobook)
ISBN 978-1-4003-3951-8 (ePub)
ISBN 978-1-4003-3950-1 (HC)

HarperCollins Publishers, Macken House, 39/40 Mayor Street Upper, Dublin 1, D01 C9W8, Ireland (https://www.harpercollins.com).

Library of Congress Control Number: 2026937775

Cover Design: Jake Weidmann
Interior Design: Kristen Sasamoto

Printed in the United States of America

26 27 28 29 30 LBC 5 4 3 2 1

DEDICATION

I dedicated my last book to my whole family save one—
Eleanor Bethel, who made her blessed appearance into this world
early during the writing of this book. So, to her and to the rest of my
adorable children, as well as my beloved wife, Hannah,
I again dedicate this book . . . trusting now that the gang's all here.

And to God my Maker, whose heart I will ever
pursue and who shapes mine after His.

CONTENTS

He who works with his hands is a

LABORER.

He who works with his hands and his head is a

CRAFTSMAN.

He who works with his hands, his head and his heart is an

ARTIST.

—SAINT FRANCIS OF ASSISI

CHAPTER ONE

ENTERING IN

Caves and Cathedrals

Caves can be either a wonder or a terror depending on your perspective. As a boy I realized they are a bit of both. While in the Boy Scouts, I went spelunking with my troop. There is a network of naturally formed tunnels and caverns in southern Colorado known as Cave of the Winds that was discovered in the 1880s. Most tours are a pedestrian's stroll on lighted pathways just inside the mouth of the cave. But on this outing, we would be going deep within the bowels of the mountain, led by an expert spelunker.

Our real journey began when we turned off the main walking trail inside the cave into a hardly noticeable opening in the cavern wall. Very quickly, the passages we were in took on a very different, almost sinister feel. No longer were there placards on the wall directing us where to go or pathway lighting at our feet. Instead, we were in a gnarled and twisted chute in the earth, spiraling downward like some kind of *Alice in Wonderland* nightmare but with more mud and less light. As the floor, ceiling, and walls of the tunnel gradually converged around us, walking gave way to crouching; crouching gave way to crawling on our hands and knees. The ceiling of the tunnel continued to press on our backs till we were soon on our bellies, inching along worm-fashion through a slurry of viscous mud that seemed to ooze out of the rock itself. At one point the space was so narrow that we had to turn our heads sideways to fit our helmets through.

Our guide told us to change our breathing pattern to slow, steady, shallow breaths so we could keep our rib cages small and squeeze our bodies through the narrow passage. I was not a particularly claustrophobic kid, but at that moment my heart was pounding against the slick, cold rock that seemed to be closing in all around it.

Finally, calls of relief came from lungs that were obviously more inflated than mine. The boys ahead of me in our wormhole seemed to have come to an opening. I dug my elbows in against the rock face and wriggled my body with greater fervor through the slimy passage. The narrow tunnel gave way to a naturally formed chute about twelve feet long. In my wet and sullied state, I shot down the slide like a gleeful kid at a water park—just a mile under the earth.

After each Boy Scout took their turn down the rock slide, we all gathered at the bottom. After congratulating us on our journey, the guide told us the tunnel system we had just traversed was aptly named "the birth canal." Perhaps that is why we were drawn together like a band of brothers having all been delivered from that same rocky womb. We stood in a circle with our arms around one another's shoulders, grinning ear to ear in the collective glow of our headlamps. White and brace-laced teeth glimmered in our mud-covered faces like a vein of precious gemstones in a mine shaft wall.

As our collective jubilation subsided, our guide spoke again to explain that the birth canal leads to one of the most astounding caverns in the entire Cave of the Winds system. And with a turn of his head, the beam from his helmet lamp illuminated the glory of the place where we were standing. A massive cavern large enough to hold a small building was before us. Stalactite formations hung like opaque icicles from the ceiling. Curtain stalactites hung like frozen drapery on every wall. Cascades of polished flowstone led from the base of the walls into crystalline pools of water. Stalagmites and full columns rose from the cavern floor and had been growing there eons before the light of man ever reached them. Having just been compressed—mind, body, and soul—beneath the weight of a mountain, our imaginations struggled all the more to fathom the grandeur of that miraculous place.

That formative experience I had in the cave as a boy returned to me when I first learned how cathedrals are designed. That feeling of compression followed by expansion is intentionally built into many cathedrals. Compression begins at the doorstep. The cathedral doors are arrayed with concentric gothic arches to give the feeling as you enter that you are being compressed or *humbled* before entering into the presence of the Lord. In many ways it, too, is a birth canal of sorts as you are reborn from a dark, dreary, sinful world into a vibrant life of faith and worship. Having first been compressed in the doorway, you are then dwarfed by the architecture within, so the humility pressed upon you at the start remains with you as you proceed into the nave. Spiring pillars, stained glass, and lofted ceilings direct your eyes heavenward in a posture of praise.

In some small way, this pattern I discovered in caves and cathedrals marks my daily commute to work. The third bay of our garage serves as my woodshop. It sits catty-corner to our larger two-bay garage where we park our cars. It is late winter here in Colorado as I write this, so my shop is very cold on the regular. Each morning, I don my Carhartt coveralls; put on my flannel jacket, hat, and boots; and make my extremely short commute to work. The door from our kitchen leads into the garage.

Once through, I have to weave my way around my wife's car and between it and the line of three large trash cans in our garage—usually brimming with the week's trash and recycling. I have to awkwardly shimmy sideways, as it is too narrow to walk abreast. That shallow breathing technique I learned in the cave comes in handy here, but it is more for the smell than the squeeze. Then comes the gauntlet of bikes and strollers, which I usually have to rearrange from the way my kids last left them to the one way they can be tetrised neatly along that portion of the wall. Finally, I round the corner into my woodshop.

My shop is no grand cavern or Gothic cathedral, mind you. Instead of stalactites, wood clamps and carving chisels are suspended on racks along the pine-paneled walls. There is no stained glass to speak of, but the late-afternoon sun streams through the windows of my garage door with a heavenly glow. Fine sawdust like incense smoke traces beams of light through the air. To the average person, it probably looks like your run-of-the-mill garage workshop—the proverbial "man cave"—but to me it is a place of wonder. Daily I am reborn into the nave of my carving studio to enter into a posture of praise. Coveralls and a waxed canvas apron serve as my liturgical vestments in that holy place. And with hands folded around the grip of a carving chisel, I join with the Spirit to pray my work into being. I am currently working on a massive wood sculpture that will take the better part of two years—it has required every ounce of my skill and then some. Needless to say, my prayer life has vastly increased!

Now, do I wish from time to time that I had a stand-alone woodshop complete with central heating and devoid of the encumbering clutter, especially including our own refuse? Absolutely! But had I waited on the perfect working conditions before I made a start on the greatest commission of my artistic career, then a start I might never have made. Furthermore, I have learned to embrace the compression of my pride before I step into the expansion of my craft and calling. That humility pressed upon me as I squirm past the overstuffed rubbish bins remains with me even while I work on my magnum opus.

Making a Start

Have you ever wanted to make something, anything, but you weren't sure where to begin or how? Have you had a dream of developing a skill but just never got around to it? Perhaps this book finds you in the midst of making, whether you are starting a business, growing a family, writing a novel, or finally knocking out that weekend DIY project. But now you are possibly feeling stuck. Maybe you recently finished some major endeavor: You finally got your degree, just had your last performance in that hit show off-Broadway, wrapped up your latest remodel, or completed that major consulting contract, and you are in that nebulous place of sweet satisfaction and postpartum woes, wondering what comes next.

Well, my friend, gift wrapped within the cover of this book is much if not all the advice I can offer you on your maker's journey. The tools I offer here are not shiny and new but well broken in and regularly honed on the grindstone of experience. They may not always be pretty, they may not be what you expect, but I promise you they are fit for the job.

Artist as Archetype

For years, I thought my experience and perspective as a working artist was unique in the world. It is true that making a living as an artist is difficult and therefore the number of full-time professionals in my industry is thin. I assumed that what I struggled with and learned over the course of a life's work had little bearing on anyone else's. But while we artists may be a rare bunch indeed, what we wrestle with in the throes of our vocation is anything but.

I experienced this paradigm shift while I was reading G. K. Chesterton's *The Everlasting Man*. This firebrand genius took to task the anthropologists of his day for portraying our earliest ancestor, the caveman, as a simple brute. Chesterton argued that there is no evidence to point to the caveman's brutality; instead, all that the cavemen left behind are paintings on cave walls. The only conclusion that can be made of the caveman, therefore, is that he was an artist. "Dig far enough down in the earth," Chesterton said, "and there you will find that a man has drawn a picture of a reindeer, but no matter how deep you dig you shall never find that a reindeer has drawn a picture of a man. For art is the signature of man."[1]

I guess what Chesterton and I are saying is that art is so easy even a caveman can do it! Art is not this highbrow form of creating that only the most enlightened of society can produce. It is, rather, based within the human instinct. Art is merely one example of this uniquely human ability to create, and perhaps the first we have record of, but it has manifested itself around the world, a million different ways or more, through time out of memory. An artist, therefore, serves as a good archetype of human ingenuity. So, here within these pages, I hope that my experience as an artist can be a kind of tool kit to assist you in whatever you're making as we walk together through the caves of the creative process.

My hope is that the tools I have fashioned for my own purposes may serve you in yours. Moreover, my ability to devise such tools can work as a kind of catalyst to your own ingenuity. While I look at charcoal and see an etching, you might look at a stick and see fire, or a pointy rock and see a spear. The broader application I am driving at, then, may not be the tool itself but rather the ingenuity behind the creation of that tool. In so doing, there is really no limit to how the principles within these pages can be applied.

While artistry is the easy part, the real challenges I face are turning that art into a sustainable business and supporting a family by it, working in less-than-ideal conditions, growing my skill, acquiring tools, balancing the books, working with my spouse, dealing with stress, and fighting burnout. Any of that sound familiar? People often have a romanticized idea of the life of the artist, but it shares many of the same struggles as any other. I have the freedom to create art in various dimensions, but I must live in this one.

Much like the caveman, I contend with the normal pressures of survival while I make my art. I may not have to worry about a saber-toothed tiger crouching at the door of my cave, but I do have a mortgage on that cave, taxes to file, and the occasional long-fanged critic to fend off. And there is a myriad of other monsters—business-related and otherwise—hiding in the shadows, waiting to pounce and swallow my art-making days whole.

There are emails to answer, phone calls to return, and bills to pay. Occasionally, one of our cars or major home appliances will break down, and you can almost guarantee that it will happen as soon as I lift the brush to the canvas. You might say at this point, "Wait, Jake, I thought you were a *full-time* artist." You are looking at it, baby! This is the real, unsexy part of being not just an artist but an entrepreneur—slugging it out in the trenches of the day-to-day. It may not be what you imagined, but I promise, it is real, worthwhile, and doable.

Keys to Survival

From that very real understanding, this book is a compilation of tools and techniques that I have found critical to my survival—a kind of war journal written in the trenches of making while in the heat of life's many battles. As I sat down to write this book and thought of what I would want from it as a reader, I came to the truth unvarnished. *Give me raw, straightforward advice, fresh off the working line with the grease still under its fingernails—the kind of stuff I can put right to work. Share with me the real-real. Show me where the sausage gets made. Don't dress it up, smooth it out, water it down, or sugarcoat it. Just hit me with it!*

So, my friend, that is what you are going to get. My honest advice, my hard-earned and hard-learned lessons, my tricks of the trade and rules for the road. I am generally reticent to give advice because I am very much still learning. But given that Michelangelo is credited with saying that very thing at the ripe old age of eighty-eight, "I'm still learning," I doubt that will change for me anytime soon. But even though I have not learned everything, I have still learned something. And what I have learned has not come from the sterile classrooms of academia—for as a degree in art or business goes, I have none to show. No, what wisdom I do have was gained on the battlefield of life.

The Heart of the Maker

In this book you have not only my wisdom but my heart on the page—my own maker's heart. Were I to tell you all I know and not share with you the *why* behind it, I would be cheating you out of the best I have to give. This book is chock-full of practicalities that can immediately be applied across a wide spectrum of human ingenuity, but if the proper motivation behind them is lacking, they will serve little more than your own vanity. Beyond any material fabrication, I want to teach you how to make meaning, and that comes only from your heart.

Following from Saint Francis's quote at the opening of this book, I have found when my hands, head, and heart are all employed in unison, that which I create is elevated from artifact to art. There may be times when I am merely the laborer or perhaps the craftsman, but once I have gotten my heart involved as the artist, that is all I ever want to be. Not just an artist in the colloquial sense, but as Saint Francis meant it, involving the whole of me.

Beyond getting to the heart of the matter, I want to lead you to the heart of the Maker. I have found that one of the greatest ways God is revealed to me is through me. This might sound like delusions of grandeur, but I assure you it is not. Why shouldn't God reveal Himself through me or through you, for that matter, as He does with all His creation, but especially with those who bear His image? There is an intimacy with God that comes through the act of creating. There is a point I reach in my work repeatedly where I have come to the end of myself, and that is where God shows up. At length, my heart begins to be made more in the image of His.

And all is useful to God as tools to shape me as His creation, my triumphs as well as my failures. On the one hand, I've had major breakthroughs, moments of brilliance, and smashing successes, and on the other hand, dumb ideas, poor decisions, embarrassing mistakes, and epic failures—of which there are many more of than the former. I have learned more from my failures than my successes, something I'm sure you have heard so many other people say that it almost reads like a truism. I am not sure why this universal phenomenon is so, but I hope to get to the bottom of it over the course of this book. Perhaps it is because success simply confirms our prior accomplishments, and there is not much left to glean after that.

When you succeed, it's a slap on the back and you continue on your way. When you fail, it's a gut punch that folds you over and stops you in your tracks. Maybe when you are halted thusly you take time to reflect on what brought you low. Moreover, pain has a sort of quickening effect on the senses. All I can really say is, I have taken my share of gut punches over the years, and the memory of their pain will live within these pages in the form of applied wisdom and my deeper reliance on God.

However, not all the insights I have to share are reactionary in their origin. Meaning, they are not born of some circumstance that happened to me, be it good or bad. As much as I can, I prefer to learn from *other people's* mistakes and, chiefly, their wisdom. Wouldn't you agree this is generally a prudent way of living? It is guaranteed to shorten your learning curve, lengthen your life, and save you from a lot of unnecessary pain. It grants you all the benefit of someone else's suffering without you having to take part *in that* suffering.

You might think that second- or thirdhand knowledge is not as relevant as something learned directly, as if it loses poignancy in its passing. Some might insist, and many often do, that each successive generation *automatically* knows better than the one previous and therefore has nothing to glean from the past. C. S. Lewis coined a term for this style of thinking: "chronological snobbery."[2]

Human flourishing depends in no small part on every generation building on the established wisdom of generations past, not ignoring it. Furthermore, bedrock truths within that wisdom dictate a style of living or action, and they are lovingly handed down to us by our forebearers as *traditions.* Within so many of the various art forms that I practice, deep traditions of the past guide my hand gracefully into the future. They have such power to instruct that their repercussions spill over from the craft into the rest of life. It will be my joy to share with you, dear reader, the power of these beloved traditions. And not my joy only, for each generation in its own time bears the responsibility to pass it forward, and so it falls to me.

Flint and Tinder

Now, if this artistically inclined Neanderthal is going to transfer the light of wisdom from my cave to yours, it will require more than just kindling—it needs a spark. For that, I will endeavor to inspire you. The deep truths I've gathered from my own experience and from ages past will create a nice tinderbox, but it is just dead wood if we don't put heat to it. In order to have the impetus to put these things into practice, you will need to understand the *why* behind everything I do. That is where inspiration comes in. As an artist, stirring the imagination is one of the things I relish most. But given that I typically inspire through pictures and this book has none, I will have to manage with my hands tied behind my back. Still, I shall strive to make pictures of words and evoke the subconscious with colorful rhetoric.

First, you should know that it is never just about the work. Beyond fashioning a durable art piece, my desire is to create a lasting change in people. Did the fools of the postmodernist movement who coined the term "art for art's sake" realize that they neutered art of its power? Art was never meant merely to point back to itself. Art, in its highest function, was always meant to lead us to something higher. A pretty picture can fill an empty wall space and a clever design can trick the eye, but my aim is the heart. If I want to create truly earth-shattering works, then they must be able to shift the tectonic plates of your soul. Does my goal sound grandiose or quixotic to you? It should! Because here's the deal, and lean in close for this one: *It's never about me either!*

Art was not intended to point to itself, and neither was I. I alone cannot transform the souls of men—that is God's business. I work in the archival; He works in the eternal. I merely set the scene in anticipation that He will take the stage. It is not a matter of inviting God into my work—He has already invited me into His. With the meager tools in my hands and nothing more, I have been given a role in His kingdom. Precisely how I join God in His work will take the entirety of this book, but I draw your attention to it here so that you will be looking for it.

So come, you artists, makers, and performers. Come, you influencers, entrepreneurs, and leaders. Come, you architects, engineers, and DIYers. Come, you mothers and fathers, creators of family and makers of home. We shall carry on the fight of creating as man has done since the dawn of time. Boldly I will lead you into the dark. Together we will sharpen our spears against outside enemies that devour ambition and courage. We will traverse the deep crevasses of the soul—those tight spots of self-doubt that catch us up and hold us fast. We will shore up the tunnel walls against the exterior pressures. We will learn to strike the spark of inspiration even when the wind blows in our faces—and carry its flame deep into the untold places of discovery. This is where we will leave our mark on the world. This is our cave of wonders. And the glory of God lies within!

CHAPTER TWO

PRACTICE

Progress over Perfection

We have all heard the adage "practice makes perfect." Perhaps a more accurate phrase is "practice makes progress." First of all, perfection is a truly lofty idea if we are not being hyperbolic. Perfection is to the maker what the North Star is to the traveler; it is to be ever pursued but never reached. They may navigate by the North Star but do not dream of getting to the star itself. Should I ever think I have arrived at perfection in my own work, then the game is up. It would be better to stop once I have achieved perfection and never create again. Well, I have not reached perfection, and so I will remain ever in pursuit of it.

The Killing Stroke

We have all heard it said that the pen is mightier than the sword. Well, perhaps never before or since has that old axiom been put to the test as it was when two dueling Master Penmen crossed quills. Their names were Louis Madarasz and Francis Courtney. These two penmen stood head and shoulders above all others for their penmanship prowess. Courtney had earned the nickname "the Pen Wizard," for what he did at the end of a pen was pure magic. He was quite the showman and liked to demonstrate his powers in scriptological sorcery any chance he got.

Courtney was ambidextrous and would begin writing a sentence with one hand and then finish it with the other. Or he would write a word upside down and backward and then twist the page around to show the perfect specimen of that particular script. He was an itinerate teacher of penmanship and traveled around the country sharing his profound wisdom of writing wizardry. To capture the imagination of his students, he would fill an entire chalkboard with museum-worthy flourishing and script. And when he was finished, he would take a piece of chalk in each hand and sign his name in opposite directions as if he were conducting an orchestra.

Louis Madarasz was hailed "the King of Penmen." He was not as flashy or bombastic as Courtney, perhaps, but he never put a stroke wrong. His command over the pen was absolute. His severe writing angle, dramatic line variation, and whisper-thin hairlines proved that he ruled over writing with a firm but steady hand.

A friendly rivalry developed between Courtney and Madarasz

over the years, and whenever the two should meet, a gauntlet of ink was thrown down. On one such occasion the two were seated on opposite sides of a table, pens drawn. And so it was in the days of yore when writing reigned, the king and the wizard came to do battle. Courtney plunged his pen into the inkwell and drew first blood. With a graceful wave of his pen staff, he performed his spellbinding magic and laid down a few words of *inkantation.* He then slid the sheet of paper across the table at Madarasz with a flourish and said, "Accomplish that, if you can." The script was exemplary, to be sure. A lesser penman would have accepted defeat at the skillful hands of the old wizard. But as legend has it, the coolheaded king picked up the paper calmly and studied the script till the ink dried on the page. And without a word, he turned the paper over, dipped his pen into his inkwell, and wrote not a word, but a single letter of surpassing beauty and utter perfection. He then slid the paper back to Courtney and said, "Accomplish *that* in a lifetime!"

I have heard the importance of practice stressed time and again. From drawing to painting to sculpting, practice, as they commonly say, is paramount. But those mediums can generally be teased along, and there is much room for forgiveness in them. A drawing can be erased, a painting can be gone over in successive layers of paint, and a clay sculpture can be reworked ad infinitum. But when it comes to the written word, you've got only one shot. Each letter should be executed fluidly. The well-practiced penman should be able to strike the page with the unforgiving pen without thought or hesitation. Madarasz always said writing requires bravery. But courage for the fight is found only in the training arena. Of all my art forms, there is none that requires as much regimented repetition as calligraphy. Only in penmanship did I finally learn the full meaning of practice.

Until You Can't Get It Wrong

In calligraphy there came a point when I could nail the letterform of a particular script but only every so often. There is a bit of a false summit when it comes to practicing each new skill, and surpassing that is when you finally begin to get it right. You might feel as though you have arrived, but you still have quite a climb ahead of you, and the progress is hard-fought and hard-won in the final ascent. Real proficiency does not mean you can get an action right some of the time or even most of the time; it means you get it right every time. Don't just practice it till you get it right; practice till you can't get it wrong.

You may have heard of the term "muscle memory." While there is some debate over the semantics of this term, by and large it is a misnomer. There is actually no memory stored in the muscles themselves. You may develop and hone your muscles for a particular act like sports or dancing, playing musical instruments, or, yes, calligraphy, but the special coordination of those muscles for such tasks are indeed stored in the brain.

While neurological science has not pegged down exactly where such information is stored, what researchers have found is an increase in white matter in the brains of those who have developed highly specialized movements. By and large, the core of the brain is made of white matter whereas the outer portion of the brain is gray matter, although there is some integration throughout. It seems that white matter is the place where special connections are made, and the physiological structure of the brain is changed with long-term, repeated practice.

Think about learning a new action and how hairy it feels at first. Your brain is having to work to make connections to seamlessly execute an action. It must somehow create a new pathway through a dense forest of neurons. Coordinating the sequence of muscles contracting and expanding in the right order and at the right time is a lot of work at first. But if you have ever developed a skill, such as learning how to dance or play an instrument, then you have experienced the phenomenon of that same awkward action becoming second nature over time. Like becoming fluent in a language, you no longer have to think about what you are saying—you just say it.

The same follows when you become fluent in an action; you no longer think about the movement—you simply move. All that practice has cleared a path and laid a highway to that action. Getting there before required a lot of cognitive maneuvering through the forest of neurons in your mind, but now you are driving on the autobahn. I think this is where the misnomer of muscle memory originated. You do not feel like your brain is involved at all; you can feel the motion in your limbs before you move them. The impressive thing is that you *are* thinking. The thought has just become so second nature to you that it feels effortless. Both your muscles and your brain have been reshaped by practice.

Don't Practice Mistakes

If practice is literally ingraining the action in your brain, you can see how critical it is to make sure you are practicing the *right* actions. If you do not check your form repeatedly, it is easy to fall into bad habits. As soon as you adopt that poor action into your practice and repeat it ad nauseam, the same transformation of the brain can happen for ill as it does for good. If you practice your mistakes, you will execute them perfectly every time with astounding proficiency. But that is not the kind of accuracy you are going for. It is possible to unlearn a bad habit, but it is very hard to do. It is far easier to correct small mistakes and further hone your skill so long as you make course corrections toward the right direction rather than backtracking over the wrong one.

Every craft in creation and every discipline in life benefits from practice. We truly are creatures of habit, and there is power to be gained from developing the right habits and ridding ourselves of the wrong ones. The best practice accomplishes both simultaneously.

Ten Thousand Hours *Plus*

Malcolm Gladwell made famous the ten-thousand-hour rule in his book *Outliers*. He posited that roughly ten thousand hours was the time required to master a skill. However, further research in this area has revealed some caveats to this rule. Mainly, what the findings show is that the *quality* of the practice matters a great deal. You may practice mindlessly for ten, twenty, or fifty thousand hours and still be relatively novice. What really produces mastery at the end of ten thousand hours is an unceasing push for improvement over that time.

Rather than just going through the motions over and over, you must think about how each of those motions can be improved on since the last time you went through them. This heightened level of focus on the minutiae of your skill brings a deeper level of mindfulness to your craft overall. As nice as it may sound to simply go into autopilot for ten thousand hours and come out the other side a master, I'm afraid it is not as easy as that. In fact, when you reach a certain level of proficiency in your skill, improvement is very hard to come by. You need to push hard to achieve those incremental gains in your skill. And this is how you ensure that you really are a master at the end of ten thousand hours.

Penmen of old already understood this intuitively, and so they stressed to their students the importance of studying as much as you practice. Meaning, no matter how proficient you become in your skill, you still need to revisit the exemplars for continued guidance. It is all too easy to fall in love with the writing coming off your pen when your skill reaches a certain level. I have seen many people do this, and even I have fallen victim to it myself from time to time. Don't get me wrong. It is a good thing to delight in your own work. In the story of creation, God looked at what He created and saw that it was *good* (Genesis 1:4, 10, 12, 18, 21, 25).

And a more rigorous interpretation of the original Hebrew text translates as not merely good but *beautiful*, which gives a yet higher declarative quality over God's work. We can and should experience something similar, albeit on a micro, human scale. But one of the major differences between our creation and God's is that ours can always and ever be improved on. If we do not study exemplars to find where we can improve, we run the danger of practicing mistakes and ingraining them in our minds. Again, it is far easier to learn a new skill than it is to correct a bad one.

A Forever Student

My wife, Hannah, and I created a jewelry brand called Everyday Heirloom Co. I will not take the time to rehash that whole start-up story, but if you're interested you can find it in my first book, *Old Soul, New Creation*. I will, however, share some inside baseball on the actual skill I had to acquire in order to start and grow that business.

For years, I had admired the skill of hand engravers for the fineness and beauty of their work. I had seen some jewelry engravers make beautiful cuts in metal using a pneumatic hand piece on a rotating vise called a graver's block. The whole art form fascinated me, and I knew that I would love to get into it if opportunity ever allowed for it. I also knew I was too busy and needed to focus on other work.

One thing I have come to learn is that when you make a living doing what you love, then doing what you love needs to make you a living. Since I knew I would never take the time to learn hand engraving properly if it was not contributing to our income somehow, I took the plunge and declared it a new business venture! I bought some engraving equipment before I really knew what I was going to do with it. But I convinced myself and Hannah (though less so) that I would find some great things to engrave and eventually sell.

When I finally got all the equipment set up and started using it, I was in a bit of a nervous panic with how foreign it all felt. I found that engraving was far more difficult than I had imagined, and my first results were genuinely a train wreck. First of all, you are supposed to hold the engraving tool like a computer mouse, with your forefinger resting on top of the engraver's chisel. The handle is planted into the palm of the hand, and there is a small pressure plate on the end that, when squeezed, activates the pneumatic piston like a gas pedal and drives the sharpened tip through the metal.

The jewelry piece is secured in the engraver's vise, which is shaped like a big metal ball. It sits in a plastic doughnut-shaped base, which allows the vise to tilt in a wide range of angles. The ball is also divided around its hemisphere with bearings, called its crown, giving the engraver the ability to twist and pivot the jewelry piece in any direction. Engraving is such fine work that you must look through a stereo microscope to see what you are doing. You are looking straight forward through the lenses, and a prism bends the focal angle down onto the engraver's block.

The tips of the engraver's chisels have to be sharpened to exact geometry, with multiple bevels ground to fractions of a millimeter wide. If the shape or sharpness of the chisel tip is off even slightly, it will wildly affect its cutting ability and performance.

When I first sat down to engrave, I found the whole action extremely disjointed. I had to push and roll the engraving tool in my right hand while twisting the engraver's block with my left hand, all the while trying to keep the jewelry piece in view through the lenses of a high-powered microscope. At such a high magnification, my depth perception was completely off, and I had a really hard time even getting my chisel tip where I wanted it to go.

After cutting just a few practice lines, the tip of the graver chipped off and I had to stop what I was doing and resharpen it all over again. I remember feeling overwhelmed in that moment and wondered if I had made a huge mistake by investing so much into equipment I didn't know how to use. After years of being well practiced in all my other art forms and enjoying the confidence that proficiency brings, all at once I was a humble student again.

When Hannah gave me my first assignment as her jeweler-for-hire, she brought me a tiny disc-shaped charm and asked me to engrave a single script initial on it. It sounded simple enough, but it was my sink-or-swim moment. Either I was going to master this thing or it was going to master me. Finally, after much practice, I was able to scribe something that looked like an actual letter. Most importantly, Hannah was satisfied.

Soon I was good enough at engraving the small letter pendants that we were able to offer them for sale. Like a preschooler learning the alphabet, I could write letters but not words. It was time to get back to class.

At length, I learned how to translate the strokes of the calligraphy pen into cuts with the graver. One form of calligraphy I am most proficient in is called engraver's script, because it was first developed for engraving into copperplates before it was translated into a writing style. I was reversing the order. I was able to do small words at first . . . then longer ones . . . then short phrases. My coordination with the handpiece and the graver's block was improving so much that I began scribing small designs, the first being a small honeybee onto a hexagonal-shaped pendant. Then I went after a signature staple of every engraver that is worth their salt—scroll leaves.

I was producing necklaces one at a time. At that point we were not limiting the number of each design for sale, and the orders would pile up. I let our business drive my practice. I would have a slew of the same design to do in quick succession. Each time I would try to refine my approach and strive to create smoother and quicker cuts. To the naked eye, the average person could not tell the difference across a dozen of my engravings of the same kind. But under the microscope I could see my skill improving, and that was more alluring to me than the precious metal in which it was emblazed.

Furthermore, knowing that someone had paid good money for my engraving made me bring my very best. And this worked as a kind of accountability for me. Even when the going got tough, I had to keep going. Inspiration is not the only form of motivation, and when that inspiration fades, it is good to have some other force holding your hand to the grindstone.

Perhaps you have experienced this in your creating. Maybe you have taken on a commission, signed a contract, or merely promised a favor to a friend. Either way, making good on your word can oftentimes be the only thing that keeps you making at all. I would encourage you not to shrug this burden but to embrace it. Fatigue, boredom, distraction, and disillusionment regularly come to the best of us. Tethering ourselves to external commitments can hold us fast to our work through the ebb and flow of our internal motivations.

I approached the craft of engraving relatively late in my career. Uncomfortable as it was initially, returning to the role of student turned out to be more exhilarating and rewarding than I ever could have imagined. I not only gained a new skill, and thereby a new outlet to express my artistic vision, but also repostured myself toward my other mediums. As I returned to painting, sculpting, and calligraphy, I was poised to learn again. Engraving had reawakened me to the power of practice!

As if that weren't enough, I learned things from engraving that carried over into my other work. For instance, the method of engraving the acanthus leaf radically changed the way I drew them in calligraphic illuminations and carved them in wood; they adorn this book *and* my last one. I once heard an old designer say that if you can draw scroll leaves well, you will never starve. I have found that to be true, as scroll leaves have become a sort of bread and butter in my pantry of artistic motifs. And it would never have been as well stocked today had I not tilled the soil of my skill, planted the seed of inspiration, and irrigated that crop with a lot of diligent practice.

Consider what learning a new discipline or skill might do in your own form of making. Maybe there is a specialty you have always admired from a distance but never given yourself the time or freedom to explore. For Hannah, it was gardening. While she had always dreamed of building her own garden from scratch in our backyard, she never realized how it would transform her cooking. As a homesteading horticulturist, she now has a deeper understanding of her ingredients, having cultivated them from planting pot to cooking pot. She can tell you the subtle difference in flavor between thyme and lemon thyme. She can tell you how harvesting her tomatoes at various stages of ripeness will determine how she will prepare them and in what recipe they are best suited.

Particular ingredients play a more central role in her dishes due in part to the season of their bloom as well as Hannah's pride in having grown them from seed.

You should not think of learning something that is so far outside your wheelhouse that it does not immediately relate to what you do. Pick something that is adjacent to your main area of expertise or something that will complement it well. Springboard off what knowledge you already have to give yourself some momentum into the unknown. If you are a musician, consider adding a new instrument to your repertoire, but don't try to jump from the piano to the didgeridoo. Pick your new instrument in relative proximity to your first. If you are an author, don't try to jump from historical nonfiction to slam poetry or the beats will have you beat before you can get back on your feet and you'll be takin' penicillin for the illin' that you feelin' and after all that practice you'll think, *Dang! I should have stuck to Erasmus!*

In our current age, specialization is greatly stressed. The world wants you to become an expert in one particular thing and to remain in that box. There is certainly some power to specialization, but I fear the idea has become too narrow. Becoming overly specialized can stunt creative growth. I once heard of a president of a company who was struggling to figure out why their business had plateaued. He had the data in front of him in the quarterly profit and loss reports, but the numbers could show him only so much; he could not discern the *why* behind them. He had tried everything he could from his high administrative post, but nothing seemed to move the needle. So, he decided to leave the confines of his office and work for several weeks in various positions on the factory floor. Becoming more familiar with the various stages of their product's development all the way through to shipping, he was able to identify many inefficiencies that bogged down the production line. After implementing changes at all the key points in the process, the business became much more efficient and the profit margins grew considerably. Becoming well practiced in any discipline means growing knowledge and skill not only in depth but in breadth as well.

Descending from the heights of expertise to novice again can be a scary descent. But what it does to shake up your mindset is life-giving in the end. You will never reach true mastery if you are not willing to become a student continually.

A Well-Practiced Heart

As you can see, practice is more than just a pastime; it is a way of life. We are all creatures of habit at our core, and the evidence is even in the wiring of our brains.

Now that we have explored at length the effect practice has on the mind of the maker, let us turn now and discuss its impact on the heart. I have found that dedicated practice serves to steady, equip, and humble the heart before entering into creation.

Practice establishes a regimen of movement to which the heart matches pace. I can feel my heart rate slow after just a few minutes of calligraphy warm-ups. My favorite strokes, like the falling spiral or the figure eight, bring my heart and hand into synchronization. Even most machines take time to warm up. And you are not a machine. You are a person, and you cannot begin from a cold start. Practice greases the wheels of your creativity. Motion is lotion to the muscles, joints, nerves, and neurons.

Whenever I try to skip out on practice, I pay dearly for it in the end. I might be in a rush to get something done and so I jump right into the work. I might have a deadline looming or I might be trying to shoehorn some work in between personal commitments. I am often guilty of packing my schedule such that I allow time enough for the actual production but little else. Often I am just so anxious to get started that I forsake my warm-up. But because I have not taken the time to calibrate my heart for the task that is before it, the art suffers. A kind of snowball effect ensues as the heart does not see what it wants from the hand. I end up making mistakes; tensions rise; I make more mistakes; I force production along. The resulting creation does not look like an expression of the heart but a contrivance of the will—and a stubborn one at that.

Practice, therefore, needs to be not only a dedicated time to build your skill but a ritualistic commencement at the start of every creative endeavor. It will not feel like a delay or added task so long as you adopt it as part of your overall method. Your heart will thank you for it and your work will exude peace and tranquility as a reflection of the spirit in which it was created.

Equipped to Serve

Practice provides a means by which the heart is known. You should not practice merely to acquire skill. And you should not acquire skill merely to impress your fellow man and win praise. More than making you skillful, practice equips you to communicate more readily and to better love others through your work. If what you make is your unique voice in the world (and it is), then practice is the means by which you hone your message, increase your vocabulary, and refine your eloquence. As the Scripture says, be ready to give an answer for the hope that lies within you (1 Peter 3:15). There is a preparedness that comes from practice. Your life's message might carry the central truths of the gospel, or it might be that middle space that the ancients used to refer to as common grace.

Either way, what you do says something about you whether you intend it to or not.

Given that people will take what they will from the message of your making, why wouldn't you lean in and take control of the narrative? As much as others may invest themselves in your message, they want to experience you as the primary shareholder. Putting in the practice is your sweat equity. God is revealing Himself to you by the desires He has put in your heart. What we create are like the divining rods that lead us to that living water of the Holy Spirit. Private practice is the ideal time to explore just what it is that God has put on your heart. Let it be yours first and only in that moment before you share it with others. Growing our aptitude and sensitivity to our craft by way of practice draws us into deeper intimacy with God. He will ultimately reveal what we have practically stumbled on. Showing up day after day and hour after hour displays not merely a commitment to our craft but a devotedness to our calling.

Talent alone cannot get the job done—it requires tactics. You may be naturally gifted, you may have profound creative insight, or you might have a grand vision for what you want to make, but none of that matters if you don't know how to put it down on paper. Tactics are the practical know-how; they are the means by which your maker's heart is known and its talent realized.

Repeatedly Humbled

Practice provides humility. I have found over the course of my life that the most technically skilled practitioners of their craft are often the humblest. I have no way to substantiate my claim other than my real-life experience. There are exceptions to this rule, of course, but on average I have found that artists who are at the top of their game and produce the highest-quality work are approachable, amicable, complimentary, and generous.

Yet I have found the ones who are deficient in skill seem to overcompensate with a surplus of ego. I have always speculated that the discrepancy between the skilled and unskilled comes down to the fact that practice has a profound ability to keep the ego in check. I think this is due in part because all work keeps women and men honest to their own limitations. So, one of the greatest effects of practice is not only to hone your skill but to cultivate your character. And so I say: Bring forth a deluge of practice over my maker's heart, and let it erode my pride!

THE DISCREPANCY BETWEEN THE SKILLED AND UNSKILLED COMES DOWN TO THE FACT THAT PRACTICE HAS A PROFOUND ABILITY TO KEEP THE EGO IN CHECK.

Practice does show gradual improvement, but it also chronicles my faults. A page or so into calligraphy practice and I may feel as though I have finally arrived at the ideal letterform I was striving for. But as I look back a dozen letters or so at an earlier variant of far lesser quality, I remember thinking the same then as I do about the last letterform. At once I realize just how deluded I was to think that I had arrived at that previous mark. Then comes the creeping thought, *Am I deluded now? Will I still regard this recent letter so perfect in a dozen more hence? Or a hundred? Or a thousand?* At that point I have only begun to realize how blind I have been to my errors. The stain of my flaws requires far more rigor than I imagined. Practice is my rinse-and-repeat.

After I have rehearsed my skills enough that they are ready for the big show, the heavy dose of humility I swallowed in private becomes my elixir against self-pride, which public praise inspires. The audience doesn't know that I was not always capable of such skillful feats, but I do. The audience doesn't know how many times I failed before I finally got it right, but I do. The audience did not have to suffer the hours of my practice, but I did. And that is my real gift to them. I languished long in the centrifuge of practice to distill the very best in me for their sake. My head bent low in the throes of practice postures my heart in penitence. I have made amends of my failures and folly. I have been refined not only for my benefit but for the benefit of all. I come to the altar bearing the best fruits of my labor.

As the nineteenth-century Scottish preacher Andrew Murray wrote, "A lesson of deepest importance is that the only humility that is really ours is not the kind we try to show before God in prayers, but the kind we carry with us, and carry out, in our ordinary conduct. The seemingly insignificant acts of daily life are the tests of eternity, because they prove what spirit possesses us."[1]

To linger on the topic of humility a bit longer, let me stress the importance of always offering your work in this manner. Nothing can spoil a beautiful gift of creation like the hubris of the giver. You might be proud of your work and want to boast in your accomplishments, but snuff out that destructive fire before it spreads. If your work is not received in the way you hoped it would be, no manner of puffery will save it—it will only kill it stone-dead. Believe me, I have made this mistake many times before. Should I find myself arguing with my audience to make them see the brilliance of my design, I know I've missed the mark, and I miss it further by arguing. My outspoken pride is the death knell that rings out over my lifeless creation.

Offer your work, then, with open hands, quiet lips, and a contrite heart. If your work is praiseworthy, let others praise it, but keep your tongue only for gratitude. By praising yourself you not only look like a pompous ass, which is repellent enough, but you also rob the viewer of their participatory role in your creation. You turn what should be an exchange into a feedback loop. And like feedback through a PA system, your prideful shrieking will have people wincing and grabbing at their ears.

IF YOUR WORK IS PRAISEWORTHY, LET OTHERS PRAISE IT, BUT KEEP YOUR TONGUE ONLY FOR GRATITUDE.

"Let another praise you, and not your own mouth; a stranger, and not your own lips" (Proverbs 27:2). Offering your work humbly is a further grace to the recipient. Receive praise graciously, and when appropriate pass it along to those who aided you in your creation. No matter what you have made, you have never once done it by your own strength. So, when you practice your skill, make it a practice in humility as well. It might seem a trivial thing, but such is the way spiritual virtues take root in us, by permeating even the most mundane aspects of our lives.

Stay the Course

Remember, we are travelers in pursuit of the North Star. Practice is not a brief jaunt down the road but a lifelong journey that goes ever on and on, making progress toward perfection. Let us be perpetual pupils that we may master our mediums. Let us exalt in the monotony of the daily grind, knowing that it not only adds tactics to our talents but also yields a steadiness, readiness, and humbleness of heart. Yes, the road will be long and hard, but we are striving for accomplishments of a lifetime. We have put in the work. We have put in time to the tune of ten thousand hours and more besides. We have earned our stripes of bravery in the training arena and we are poised to create! So come, inspiration, and stir our maker's heart to making!

CHAPTER THREE

INSPIRATION

Striking a Spark in a Hurricane

When it comes to the idea of striking a spark in a hurricane, I cannot think of a more fitting example than the present, for I am in the eye of a hurricane now. *Insert thunderclap.* Imagine me as one of those pitiable field correspondents who report live from the center of a natural disaster. Picture me as those reporters always are—shouting into the camera through a deluge of horizontal rain and gale-force winds while wearing little more than a poncho. Watch on with a sort of morbid curiosity as the floodwaters of my circumstance rise and threaten to sweep me off my feet.

Coming to you live from inside the storm!

I am in the process of launching my first book while writing this, my second. Simultaneously, I am working on the largest art piece of my career, which involves separately carving some twenty different pieces of wood and assembling them into a family crest that will stand five feet tall. I have three children under eight, and my wife is expecting our fourth in a matter of weeks if not days. The Doppler radar of my life shows an incoming system of speaking engagements and podcast interviews owing to the launch of my new book, converging with a stream of midnight feedings and diaper changes in what is bound to be the *perfect storm*. To add to the level of precipitation in my life, I have also been in a monthslong spat with our HOA over a lovely garden shed we are building on our property. I am convinced there is nothing that will snuff out the spark of inspiration quicker than the wet blankets currently occupying our HOA board.

Do you remember that scene from *The Wizard of Oz* when Dorothy runs inside her house looking for her Auntie Em in the middle of a Kansas windstorm? She's knocked out cold when a window is blown in and smites her on the back of her head. When she comes to, she finds that she is aloft inside her house, swirling around in a tornado. As Dorothy looks out the window, she sees many a peculiar passerby seemingly oblivious to the fact that they are caught up in the same twister. This scene shares some eerie similarities with my current state of mind. I see my wife and kids, I see art pieces, my books, and house projects on regular rotation in the whirlwind of my mind.

Trying to find a moment of solace to create beautiful art in this torrent of life is not for the faint of heart. I may eventually land on the other side of the rainbow, but the work cannot wait. I must begin now.

Banging Rocks

So, to the question at hand: How do you strike a spark in a hurricane? Well, before we get to the inclement weather, we first need to address the striking of the spark itself. And for this, let us return to our example of the caveman from the first chapter.

Humanity's earliest exposure to fire is believed to have been when dry lightning struck the landscape and ignited a blaze. What a mystical wonder this must have been to prehistoric people, to see that jagged bolt of burning light shoot from ominous clouds and enchant the earth with billowing smoke and glowing flame. How long it took our ancestors to make use of this fire is anyone's guess. Likewise, exactly when and how humans acquired the ability to make such fire themselves is beyond the reach of history. But what is generally speculated is that one of humanity's greatest and most important achievements happened quite by accident.

Since prehistoric times, humans have made stone tools through a process called flintknapping. This Stone Age technique can be rather sophisticated in its execution. The exact process of how some of these specimens were made still baffles anthropologists to this day. Arrowheads come in a variety of shapes and sizes. Some points have serrations, notches, flutes, and barbs. The flintknapper must have a deep understanding of the type of stone they are using and how it will flake and fracture. Materials like chert, obsidian, and flint make for the most workable stones. These materials also happen to be very high in silica content, which makes them effective at producing sparks.

It is believed that in the course of flintknapping an arrowhead or spearhead, humans at some point struck one rock with another and . . . *Eureka!* There in the midst of the mundane, the miraculous was achieved. At the very fingertips of some distant caveman hard at work was struck the tiniest bolt of lightning—a spark!

There is a deep lesson to be learned from the caveman, and in a statement widely attributed to Pablo Picasso: "Inspiration will come but it must find you working."

Too often I have heard artists say that they sit and wait for inspiration to come before they start creating. Patiently they wait for the conditions to be right: for the clouds to build, the particles to collide, and the lightning to finally strike. It is a romantic notion but hardly a practical one. I am not sure where those artists are now, but I doubt they are still making art—at least not professionally. For all I know they are still sitting there, waiting with their eyes to the sky and their hands in their lap. If you wait for inspiration to come, you might be waiting an awfully long time.

Imagine a wedding photographer who had to wait for the right inspiration before capturing the lovely couple on their wedding day. What if she was still pining for motivation at those critical moments like the kiss at the altar or the cutting of the cake? How long would the in-laws have to stand in situ for the family portrait while waiting on her inspiration to spark and her camera to flash? The photographer might be patient enough for her passion to build, but I doubt the bride and groom would be. And that is to say nothing of the hungry wedding attendants; they might throw rice at the happy couple, but God only knows what they might throw at the photographer.

What if your local plumber had to wait for the right inspiration before attending to the leak you found coming from the upstairs bathroom? Imagine how infuriated you would be if he came into your house and sat on his toolbox like Auguste Rodin's sculpture of *The Thinker* while awaiting the arrival of his muse. What would come first, the rupture of that bubble forming in the ceiling drywall or the rapture of his plumbery passions?

Making a living from my art means that I do not have the luxury of waiting for inspiration to strike from the heavens. I have deadlines to meet, bills to pay, and other commitments to attend to. My process is slow, to be sure, and I am in no rush to make bad art, but neither am I idle. The fact that my process *is slow* means that I must be all the more diligent with my time. Slow and steady wins the race, but steadily I must keep trudging. The ability to conjure up my own inspiration or to carry on without it is paramount to my success and a hallmark of my professionalism.

MAKING A LIVING FROM MY ART MEANS THAT I DO NOT HAVE THE LUXURY OF WAITING FOR INSPIRATION TO STRIKE FROM THE HEAVENS. I HAVE DEADLINES TO MEET, BILLS TO PAY, AND OTHER COMMITMENTS TO ATTEND TO.

Honestly, there are many days that I approach the easel, drawing table, or workbench feeling utterly uninspired. The challenge of working on long commissions is that you can toil day after day with no sense of closure or accomplishment. The sculpture I am working on now, for instance, I have spent nearly two weeks carving and sanding on just the back side. It is a wall-hanging sculpture, which will be permanently installed in the client's home once it is finished. Yes, it is important that the back is contoured and undercut correctly so that the shape from the front appears light, thin, and not bulky. I could have just stopped after roughing the shape with my chisels, but I didn't. I sanded it smooth. Those two weeks of my life's work will be forever sandwiched against a wall. If you are looking for the definition of an exercise in futility, I may have just given you one.

There is a little-known mark of a good furniture craftsman that is so hidden, you have to go looking for it. Within a cabinet or dresser of quality make, you may find that the backs of the drawers are painted or stained. Why on earth, you may ask, would someone go to such lengths to finish the unseen portions of a piece of furniture? Why, it is the mark of their trade. The finishing of the cabinetry to the very last detail and to the same degree as the rest is a testament to the maker's commitment and craft. On the rare occasion that the chest of drawers may be disassembled for moving or repair, the integrity of the craftsman is revealed. Was painting the backs of the drawers the most inspiring bit of work for the cabinetmaker? Doubtful. Not all the work we do is destined for the light of praise. Yet the proofing of our creative tenacity is achieved in the unseen aspects of our work.

There are other times as well when I feel less than motivated toward my work. I might get tired of this or that medium and want to move on to something else. I may be commissioned to create something for a client but do not automatically share their passion for it. And just like you, I fight fatigue, lack of focus, hunger pangs, and boredom. But hey, tough darts! This is the job, and I am the man for it. There are many times when I have to sling my bag of woes over my shoulder and crack on with the work! At such moments I imagine my work feels not unlike the work of the caveman—just banging a bunch of rocks together. But what I have come to learn over the course of my career thus far is that so long as I keep banging at those rocks, eventually sparks will fly.

Terrible Masters

Emotions are great servants but poor masters.

—Kajana Cetshwayo

You may not *feel* like diving into your creation, but you should not let those feelings be your master. Behavioral psychology suggests that when you lead with action, emotions will follow suit. Force a smile on your face and your brain associates the contraction of those facial muscles with positive emotions, and it will thereby elevate your mood. An action that is typically reactive can be turned proactive. And herein lies the key to creative self-sufficiency. You can flip the script entirely. Either start with inspiration before the creative tasks begin. Or begin tasks creative, then comes inspiration. Do you see what I did in those two sentences? They are a literary ambigram, or mirror images of each other. The slightest mental shift such as this is all it takes to gain mastery over your creative process.

WHAT I HAVE COME TO LEARN OVER THE COURSE OF MY CAREER THUS FAR IS THAT SO LONG AS I KEEP BANGING AT THOSE ROCKS, EVENTUALLY SPARKS WILL FLY.

Too often we let the tail wag the dog when it comes to our behaviors and the corollary feelings that vacillate from them. If we are honest with ourselves, it feels good to be swept up in emotion or struck in a magical moment of inspiration. And I am not telling you to refuse those instances when they do come. On the contrary, seize those electrifying epiphanies for all they are worth. Capture that lightning in a jar! You surely don't need my advice at such times, as they are so compelling, you cannot help but respond accordingly. My one word of caution, however, is not to become dependent on such catalytic occurrences.

In his book *The Four Loves*, C. S. Lewis described falling in love like a headlong plunge into a pool. The rush of passion and adrenaline, with a little dose of angst, washes over us when we swan dive into a new love relationship. But, he said, once we are in the pool, swimming, not diving is the thing.[1] I think we approach our creative work in much the same way. Some people live for diving; these are the types who are always starting something new but give up as soon as inspiration wanes. Much like those people who love falling in love but are always in and out of relationships. No sooner will they resurface from a spectacular high dive into some new endeavor than they have clung onto the ladder out of the pool. These types are great starters and are usually quite visionary, but they lack the stamina to go the distance of that vision.

That initial momentum of inspiration's dive will last for only so long, whereas once you are fully submerged in your work, regular kicking and paddling will give you laps around the pool. And as Lewis suggested, there is a deeper joy found in the long swim than the quick jump. A flash of inspiration is incredibly invigorating when it comes, but the deeper fulfillment I get is found in the long swim of lasting work.

When the Thunder Rolls

Now that we have established that we need not be dependent on outside inspiration, as the power to strike a spark lies at our fingertips, let's get back to the weather.

Stoking your own inspiration is a real skill that can take some time to master. But throw in the headwind of extraneous circumstances, and now you have a fitting challenge. There have been so many times in my life when I start to see the smoke rise from my burgeoning inspiration, only to have it snuffed out by the tyranny of the urgent.

As I look back on my life, I understand how I was conditioned to view my creative endeavors—what I *wanted* to do at constant odds with what I *had* to do. For instance, I always *had to* finish my homework before I could draw as a kid. You can probably guess how often that rule was broken. (Sorry, Mom and Dad!) But even when I stole away in secret from my scholarly duties to tease along a drawing that was absolutely itching its way out of my fingertips, I did so under the constant shadow of guilt. Now, as a grown man getting paid to produce art professionally, that shadow still haunts me. My mind automatically turns to the things *I have to do* whenever I go to create. And guess what? There is always something else that *has to* be done!

Making art still feels like playtime to me—and it is very important that it remains playful. But when the house is a mess and through the walls it sounds like our sweet kids have somehow turned into a barbarian horde, and I am in my shop whittling away on a beautiful piece of timber, it feels like fiddling while Rome burns. That is precisely when I need to remind myself that I am absolutely doing the work I am supposed to. Moreover, I married a very capable woman. More than tidying the house and civilizing our children, Hannah tends to a myriad of business matters on a daily basis. At the end of the day when I knock the sawdust from my shoulders and walk in the house, I often find her cooking up a delicious dinner in our clean and beautiful home as our children are either coloring at the counter or playing peacefully in the family room. Somehow the world has been turned right side up without me.

Though storms will break eventually, they are still disruptive while they are raging. Acquiring the skill to get your creative fires lit and burning in the downpour of life is a critical tool of survival, and it requires three important steps.

Step 1: Block the Wind

A couple of weeks ago, our schedule was very dynamic, with inquiries, communications, and commitments coming in hot and heavy. My phone was blowing up with notifications of one sort or another, and it was just about driving me crazy. I kept my phone nearby in the woodshop as I worked. I like to listen to audiobooks, podcasts, or music while I am chiseling away as it occupies the other half of my brain and keeps me focused. Unfortunately, a smartphone is like the Swiss Army knife of digital tools, except it automatically flings out the saw blade, the fork, and the can opener when you are just trying to use the tweezers. It goes beyond being useful and becomes downright dangerous. Nothing can suck away my time, attention, and creativity like my phone. Its mere presence in the room is distraction enough. Various studies have proven that the majority of the engagements any user has with their smartphone is self-prompted, meaning unsolicited by notifications on the phone itself.[2] I am guilty as charged!

> ACQUIRING THE SKILL TO GET YOUR CREATIVE FIRES LIT AND BURNING IN THE DOWNPOUR OF LIFE IS A CRITICAL TOOL OF SURVIVAL.

Given all the different media and communication we consume through our devices, it is not merely a cracked door letting in a draft—it is a breach of the levy walls letting in a tsunami of distractions. After repeatedly being swept up in the chaos, I told my wife I was keeping my phone in the house as a new rule. It is no longer allowed in the woodshop.

Establishing boundaries around our creative work is critical to our productivity. Putting my phone out of reach is just one example. A boundary for you may look like a closed door, a strictly scheduled time to create, designated tools, or isolating yourself in a remote location. I have employed all the above at one point or another.

Step 2: Begin with Kindling

In order to build a roaring log fire, you cannot begin with the logs, as a rule. A key principle of fire building is that you must start with the small kindling first and build up to larger tinder. Likewise, when I create—especially from a cold start in a chaotic season—I don't try to tackle the hardest thing first; I begin with some easy wins that might catch by a simple spark. This might look like some loose practice on scrap paper before I dive back into a calligraphic illumination, or rough carving the overburden on a wood sculpture before I return to the more detailed portion where stakes are higher and a slipup could be costly. Eventually, I will be able to move on to progressively harder aspects of my work once the heat of my intensity returns. If I tried to jump to the hardest or most intense aspect of my work, I would likely intimidate myself and quit in frustration.

> ESTABLISHING BOUNDARIES AROUND OUR CREATIVE WORK IS CRITICAL TO OUR PRODUCTIVITY.

At times the "kindling" may be as small as merely *thinking* about my work long before I get there. Sports psychology research has shown a strong correlation between a player's premeditation and actual performance. Essentially, a pro athlete will get their fires smoldering long before they step on the field—indeed, they are trained to do so.

I find the more specific my premeditation is, the greater effect it will have on my state of mind. I don't just think in vague terms about painting a picture; I think about the incremental steps of getting started and the minute details of the process. I think about the colors of paint I will select from my cabinet drawers. *Will I go with cobalt blue or cerulean blue? Titanium white or flake white? Will I begin with the flat brush or the round?* I think of the smell of the paint and the feel of the loaded brush gliding across the triple-gesso-coated linen canvas. The more detailed my imagination is, the more securely anchored is my focus to the task before me.

Think about your own work. You may not be painting a canvas or stepping onto a baseball field in the major leagues. Then again, you might. Either way, all work is performative on some level, and the lessons of sports psychology can apply to you. Developing a ritual of premeditative thought around your own work can vastly improve your ability to get into it more quickly and be more effective once you are there.

DEVELOPING A RITUAL OF PREMEDITATIVE THOUGHT AROUND YOUR OWN WORK CAN VASTLY IMPROVE YOUR ABILITY TO GET INTO IT MORE QUICKLY AND BE MORE EFFECTIVE ONCE YOU ARE THERE.

Step 3: Keep Your Embers Alive

As difficult as it is to strike a spark in a hurricane, once you do have a fire going, try your best to keep it smoldering. You might have to let it burn down to embers, but it is a good idea to stoke it from time to time. Rekindling your fire takes far less energy than starting cold. What do I mean by this? Even as you necessarily step away from your work, don't wander too far from it mentally. I am not suggesting you become some kind of monomaniac, with every waking thought bent on a singular goal. Nobody likes a person who is so transfixed on one subject. You know the type: They steer every conversation back to that one thing and talk about it ad nauseam. And we are all thinking of our own example right now, as each of us has at least one of these people in our lives. Perhaps you have even played the role of the monomaniac yourself now and again—I know I have. I am not prescribing that, however.

EVEN AS YOU NECESSARILY STEP AWAY FROM YOUR WORK, DON'T WANDER TOO FAR FROM IT MENTALLY.

What I am suggesting is a healthy level of mindfulness toward your work. It is easy to distract ourselves from it so much that our passion for work dies out completely. Just as an athlete on the sidelines needs to stay loose for the moment they are called back in the game, you, too, need to maintain a kind of readiness to jump back into your own creative scrimmage. Once the coals are hot in your fire, even the strongest wind cannot blow them out.

Don't Fear the Storm

About once a month I meet with a group of friends to smoke pipes, tilt pints, and discuss philosophy, theology, and the general matters of life. We unironically call our happy gathering "Inklings," obviously modeled after Lewis and Tolkien's group of intellectuals and creators. We convene at Churchill's Bar in the historic Brown Palace

Hotel in downtown Denver. Leather-tufted couches and low-back chairs arranged around marble-topped tables line the smoke-filled room. Ornately patterned drapes fringed in golden tassels frame the leaded windows that look out on the street level of the city.

Each month, the topic du jour is determined by one of the men in the group, which centers our conversation for the evening. Last week that duty fell to me. The composition of the gathering changes month to month as commitments and calendars allow. The mix of the conclave that evening consisted of a blacksmith, a filmmaker, an entrepreneur, and me, an artist. I thought the topic of this chapter had the potential to hang in the air with the intrigue of a well-blown smoke ring. And as I packed my pipe with fragrant tobacco, I put forth the idea of striking a spark in a hurricane before the three gents, then raised the pipe spout to my lips as I let them ponder. I struck a match, a spark flashed, a flame glowed, billows rolled, and what wisdom followed from those three men that night was golden.

Each in their turn described the nature of the respective "storms" in their life and what creative measures they take to weather them. I was so grateful to have this opportunity to beta test the content of this chapter. So much of what they had to say on the matter traced the words I had already written down. Many additional thoughts I have woven back into the previous paragraphs. But one comment late in the evening coming from Jonathan, the filmmaker, seemed to bring the conversation to a decisive point. In no uncertain terms, Jon said, "We must not fear the storm"—and that statement landed with its own kind of thunderous boom.

Of course he was right! And we all agreed that the storms of life are not to be feared but embraced, for they produce in us a greater, more stalwart ability to create. Had we always gone about our business under clear skies with the sun on our backs, we likely never would have made what we did in the way that we did. Who knows.

On many occasions we may not have bothered creating at all. The hurricanes of life are uncomfortable if not terrible things to endure so long as we are in them, but one silver lining to those very dark and ominous clouds is that the fight for survival awakens within us a different kind of creative vigor. It is easy to become complacent in your skill so long as it remains merely a pastime, but when it is your livelihood—when the well-being of your family depends on it—it is called to a higher level for the greater purpose it serves.

> THE FIGHT FOR SURVIVAL AWAKENS WITHIN US A DIFFERENT KIND OF CREATIVE VIGOR.

And as to my own storm I reported on at the beginning . . . well, my first book, *Old Soul, New Creation*, has officially and successfully launched. The responses I have already received are encouraging in ways I never could have imagined, which has stirred my inspiration all the more for this book. My massive carving continues to take shape little by little, and I am enjoying it as much as I ever have. And that fourth baby I told you we were expecting—she is here and asleep on my chest at this very moment as I sit reclined on our back porch watching the sun set behind the Colorado Rockies.

So, yeah, I'd say my good friend Jon was right: I should not fear the storm—certainly not this *beautiful* storm. I am deliriously tired and busier than ever, but I would not trade it for the world. Not only are there blessings in this season that I would not wish away (for I know I will be wanting them back one day), but I can actually feel it growing me as a creator.

From Paleolithic man to Picasso, one truth remains the same: Inspiration will come, but it must find you already at work. So do not delay—begin now! Start banging those rocks together. Eventually the sparks will fly. More than what you are already making, you'll soon conjure lightning at your fingertips. So put your back to the wind and face the fire. You can't control the weather, but you can hide your flame from the tempest. Begin small. Feed your fire. Soon you'll have a bed of burning coals. The wind will howl. The cold will bite. The storm will rage on, but there in the midst you are making! Now that you have put in the practice and harnessed inspiration, it is time to let your imagination run loose and lead you to the land of ideation.

CHAPTER FOUR

IDEATION

From Musing to Making

There's gold in those hills!" High in the Rocky Mountains in Colorado lives one of the largest living organisms in the world. Kenosha Pass is home to a network of aspen trees all connected through a shared root system that spans for miles over peaks and through valleys.

Each year in the early fall, these leafy giants sprouting from the mountainside undergo a unified transformation as their foliage morphs from deep green to bright yellow. These ancient mountains have had their share of gold rushes over the centuries, but none come as often nor pay out as bountifully as the gold that grows on our trees each year. Hikers from around the state and even the country make a pilgrimage to the Rockies during this critical season to seek their fortune in the forest. Being a native of this high country and a lover of its articulated landscape, I myself have made this journey many times. Whenever I go, I always reach the pass to find that the parking lot to the trailhead is full. Not only that, but the dirt road that leads to it for a good mile or so is lined on both sides with cars—a good number of them being either Toyota 4Runners or Subaru Outbacks. A couple of years the line of parked cars strung itself clear out onto the sides of the highway before the turnoff to Kenosha.

When I eventually do find a parking spot and walk the long gauntlet of parked cars—the hike before the hike—I arrive at the trailhead and understand in an instant why the masses have been drawn here. It is a real-life enchanted forest!

Massive, spiring tree trunks animated by the mountain breeze sway slowly in unison like some ritualistic dance known only to the trees. Innumerable black, eye-shaped knots beset in the smooth, stark-white bark gaze coldly from every angle—keeping watch over the forest floor. The thick aspen canopy is arrayed with a panoply of golden medallions flickering in the sunlight against a sky of lapis lazuli. One cannot help but be awestruck from the start, but your astonishment only grows as you continue up that long, charmed trail. The subtle clapping of windblown leaves in the boughs applauds your every step.

There is one particular hike in this gilded forest I will never forget. I was with my wife, Hannah, and we had timed our arrival to Kenosha Pass perfectly. The aspens were in their peak color and had not given up their leafy fortune to Old Man Winter just yet. The air was crisp but warming slightly by the late-morning sun. Hannah and I had a wonderful hike for a couple of miles up the pass till the thick aspen forest broke around us and we came to an outcropping on the side of the mountain. From that vantage we looked out over the valley and the adjacent mountain peaks and could see nearly the entire network of aspens adorned in their seasonal vestments.

It was a sea of gold trapped in a mountain basin. For a moment the air was still, and all was quiet. Then, at a great distance we could hear a lone gust of wind moving down the peak opposite us and across the valley floor, making its way up the tree-covered mountainside where we stood. Eventually that mighty breeze broke upon us like a collective exhale of the Rockies before they settled into their long winter sleep. Hearing the wild wind's impending approach made the experience all the more exhilarating before it finally washed over us and refreshed our spirits. It was as if the very hand of God had scooped up all the oxygenated air produced by the glowing aspens and baptized us unto renewed life for the long hike back down the mountain.

In the high country of creative endeavor where golden things grow, the coming of new ideas feels a bit like this. From only God knows where, the rush and flow of generative thought comes upon me like a mountain wind. In a kind of foreknowledge I can only compare to that distant rustling of the trees in the valley, I have a preemptive notion of coming revelation before it washes over me. This is one of my favorite phases of the creative process and one that always evokes a grand sense of wonder in me. I stand on the precipice of possibility in this beautiful tension between what is *not yet* and what *could be*. For me, this is where creation begins.

Idea Maker

The goal of this chapter is to help you generate more ideas on command. You may have stumbled from time to time on that high vantage point of ideation through the forest of your mind but keep getting lost in the woods. Perhaps the bramble of self-doubt catches you up or the bunny trails of distraction lead you from your course. Our aim is to clear the trail and even establish some signposts on it as we go. Eventually, you will find your feet on a discernible path that leads straight back to the high places of generative thought where the wild wind blows.

Whether I am conjuring up the concept for a new original art piece or I am fulfilling a commission for a client, the ideation phase is always a joy to me. I love a good brainstorming session, especially with a freshly sharpened pencil, a good sketchbook, and a steaming cup of coffee close at hand. On these very special occasions, I get to unleash my imagination and let it run riot. There are no limits, no holds barred, nothing that *can't* be done. I do not think about the typical limitations of time, scope, and budget, as that would only hinder my thought process. I do not even let my current skill level or knowledge base limit me during this stage. I am chiefly focused on the *what* and the *why* . . . the *how* will have its own day. There may not be much in the way of anything tangible being formed, but make no mistake, the creative process is well underway.

If there was ever one man in history who had the profound ability of manifesting even his grandest ideas in the most solid form, it was Michelangelo. Yet as a boy, that budding Florentine sculptor had a contentious relationship with his father, which often hampered his creative flow. Utterly transfixed from a very early age on becoming an artist and carving marble, Michelangelo spent every moment he could drawing or sculpting. However, his father, Ludovico di

Leonardo Buonarroti Simoni, wanted his son to take up the family trade of small-scale banking. After a heated argument between the two, Ludovico took away Michelangelo's carving tools as punishment. Later, a friend of Michelangelo came by his family estate for a visit and found him alone in his barn just sitting and staring at a block of marble. When the friend asked Michelangelo what he was doing, he simply replied, "I am sculpting."

You may be doing little more than shifting neurons while in the ideation phase. But, according to Michelangelo, you have already started working.

This stage of creation is one in which I *feel* most like an artist. Perhaps it is because it is as close as I can get to creating as God does—*ex nihilo*, meaning "from nothing." Of course, I am still an eternity's distance from God's generative power of speaking matter into existence. I can take paper and charcoal and turn it into a drawing. I can take a roll of linen, some sticks of wood, and a few smudges of pigment and make a beautiful painting. I can take a block of wood and turn it into an ornate sculpture. But I must always begin with matter of some kind. I can make a lot from very little, but I cannot make something from nothing. And God did not just make something; He made *everything*. Even my thoughts, as original as I might think them to be, are still derivative in God's created order. And God, let them be from You, derived, and not apart from You, depraved!

YOU MAY BE DOING LITTLE MORE THAN SHIFTING NEURONS WHILE IN THE IDEATION PHASE. BUT, ACCORDING TO MICHELANGELO, YOU HAVE ALREADY STARTED WORKING.

I stress this point because there are some who like to equate man's ability to imaginatively make and God's supreme ex nihilo creation power. The danger of a culture that regularly speaks in hyperbole to emphasize a point is that exaggerations soon slip into untruths. Putting our abilities into proper perspective is not to think less of our creative powers but rather more, because it is true whereas the other way is false.

And there is still so much to marvel at without overwrought embellishment of our abilities. God has so graciously shared His creation power with us in a scaled-down version in what the theologians call a *communicable attribute*. Let us marvel at the fact that we have the ability to create at all. Let us marvel at the fact that God wanted us to share in His likeness (Genesis 1:27). And let us marvel at the fact that *the Maker's heart* is revealed in ours whenever we create.

Bezalel

One of the people in the Bible I want to meet when I pass beyond that thin veil, besides Jesus of course, is a man called Bezalel. He is a little-known character to even the most devout Bible readers, but he is a man of great import in biblical history, for he was commissioned by God to create the tabernacle. He is also the first mentioned in Scripture to receive the gift of the Holy Spirit: "The Lord said to Moses, 'See, I have called by name Bezalel the son of Uri, son of Hur, of the tribe of Judah, and I have filled him with the Spirit of God, with

THE MAKER'S HEART IS REVEALED IN OURS WHENEVER WE CREATE.

ability and intelligence, with knowledge and all craftsmanship, to devise artistic designs, to work in gold, silver, and bronze, in cutting stones for setting, and in carving wood, to work in every craft'" (Exodus 31:1–5).

When I was young and a talent for art was burgeoning in me, my father prayed that I would be a Bezalel for my generation. That was the first I had learned of Bezalel and the calling on his life as a maker before the Lord. And it was the first time his name had ever been associated with mine. Years later when I was in college, my roommate came back to the dorm straight from his Old Testament history class and told me they had just read about Bezalel, and he immediately thought of me. He stood in our entryway with his backpack still on and read the first few verses of Exodus 31. He got to the end of it and said, "Jake, that sounds just like you!"

Some years after that, when Hannah and I had just started dating, she told me one day that she felt a prompting from the Lord to read out of Exodus. She came to chapter 31. She told me on a date one evening that she read about Bezalel and felt as though the Holy Spirit had led her there for my sake, to gain further understanding of the calling that is on my life. I was quickly moved to tears. Hannah, not knowing me very well yet, thought she had maybe said something wrong. I told her not to apologize, and I filled her in on a bit more of my history. I told her that God speaks to me in threes. I am not sure if it is God's way of being romantic or symbolic as the triune God, or if I am just that hardheaded that He has to repeat Himself. Either way, I got the message.

Ever since then, Bezalel has been a hero of the faith for me as the first Spirit-filled maker. I want my life to be modeled after his. I want to hear from the Spirit the way he did. I want to be gifted by God the way he was. And why not? We may be thousands of years apart on the timeline of history, but we serve the same God.

But not only me—I want there to be many Bezalels in each generation, all gifted by God and hearing from the Lord as to what He would have us create. As much as I want this, I believe God wants it more. I have already had the pleasure of meeting spiritual sons and daughters of Bezalel. I have been ministered to greatly by the skill God has put in their hands and in their hearts. Just as the tabernacle is patterned after the kingdom of heaven, those precious creators are establishing God's kingdom here on earth. And I invite you to join them. Yes, you, dear reader! I don't know what gifts God has put in you, but they will find no higher calling than when you return them back to Him for His good purposes. He is ready and willing to equip you. It doesn't matter your age or expertise. He longs to transform your maker's heart into His tabernacle!

So, when it comes to ideation, I especially want to have an ear to the Lord. I want my maker's heart to be filled with His Spirit every time I am called to create so that I am aligning myself with His will and not my own. I know not every creative engagement will bring heaven to earth, but I still want to create as unto the Lord. Outside of being one of the early apostles for Christ and spreading the gospel, Saint Paul also worked a day job as a tent-maker. Some days I am making *tents* and some days I am building *tabernacles*.

Begin with What You Know

Different from the other stages of making, here I am beginning from scratch. I wish I could tell you that I always have the same process for concept generation, but given the variety of work that I do, the process is rarely ever the same. I do, however, have a few favorite ways to begin my quests. I think of them like the base camp at

Mount Everest. Like the mountain climber, I may not have my exact route planned all the way up my prospective mountain of achievement, especially given eventualities that I cannot account for, just like the mountaineer cannot account for the weather. But *base camp* is where I get acclimated to the elevation of my looming creation. One base camp for me is to begin with what I know, regardless of how trivial it might seem.

A faun with an umbrella carrying packages in the snow—that was the first inkling that came to C. S. Lewis years before he ever made a start on his famous series, *The Chronicles of Narnia*. Like a familiar tune that rang in his head, the image of the faun kept returning to him before he finally decided to sit down and build a story around it—and oh, what a story! That grand series beloved by children and grown-ups alike all began from a simple, obscure, imaginative thought that was even less than a daydream.

I could hardly believe that was all Lewis started with when I first learned of this from his own writings. Surely, scholar that he was, Professor Lewis must have begun with a carefully outlined plot or the development of major characters, exploration of central themes, or pages and pages of backstory. Nope—just a faun in the snow. Oh, don't forget the umbrella and the packages, of course. Yes, so much to go on! As much as I wanted to doubt it, Lewis himself said that was his starting point. In hindsight, and with *The Chronicles of Narnia* having cemented itself in the literary world as an enduring classic, it's almost as if one of Lewis's characters had traveled through time to beckon him into the formation of the epic tale. It was as if Mr. Tumnus had popped through the wardrobe of Lewis's imagination to invite him not just to visit Narnia but to create it!

I love this story from Lewis, as it is proof that ideas can come from anywhere and lead to just about anything. Ideation is that critical start to the creative process. Long before our ideas take shape and make their way out into the world, they bubble up from somewhere inside us. Our ideas may come as a crystal-clear epiphany or a vague inclination. Becoming an effective and well-practiced creator means that we must create a well-worn path in our minds from ideation to creation.

Don't Say No

BECOMING AN EFFECTIVE AND WELL-PRACTICED CREATOR MEANS THAT WE MUST CREATE A WELL-WORN PATH IN OUR MINDS FROM IDEATION TO CREATION.

Whether you are dreaming alone or brainstorming in a group, the most assured way of halting the free flow of ideas is by saying no. Refuting any notions that come up at this stage is bound to stop them altogether. There will be plenty of time for refinement or out-and-out elimination later, but *not* during the ideation phase. Leave your criticisms at the door. Beyond not saying no, you need to also remove negative words like *can't*, *won't*, or *shouldn't*.

The heart of the maker is vulnerable during the ideation phase because it is opening itself up to dream. Think of the maker's heart like a sea anemone at this stage. It is in full bloom with all its fragile tentacles sifting the current for possibilities. The hidden ambitions of the heart are exposed and there is a tacit admission that something is lacking, whether it is time, resources, or skill—all vulnerabilities are laid bare. The slightest disturbance will cause it to close in on itself to protect its most fragile parts.

Simple words like *can't*, *shouldn't*, or the simplest of all, *no*, can cut like a knife. A defeatist mindset can easily take over and cause the heart to close up again with its hopes, dreams, and ambitions still locked inside. I am reminded here of a short poem by W. B. Yeats:

> Had I the heavens' embroidered cloths,
> Enwrought with golden and silver light,
> The blue and the dim and the dark cloths
> Of night and light and the half-light,
> I would spread the cloths under your feet:
> But I, being poor, have only my dreams;
> I have spread my dreams under your feet;
> Tread softly because you tread on my dreams.[1]

Treading softly is exactly what is called for when someone has spread their dreams beneath your feet. You may have good intentions and only desire to help. You might want the dreamer to think rationally, but when is dreaming ever rational? Rationality sees only what is, whereas dreaming sees what is not yet and what could be. Dreaming secures one's hopes in the future; it teaches the heart not to succumb to the opportunities of the moment but to suffer long for the greater promises of tomorrow. Even constructive criticism tromps like dirty boots on the silken cloths of the dreamer. Better you should remove your sullied footwear before setting foot on that holy ground.

> THE HEART OF THE MAKER IS VULNERABLE DURING THE IDEATION PHASE BECAUSE IT IS OPENING ITSELF UP TO DREAM.

Of course, you can play both the dreamer and the dream crusher at the same time. We are all familiar with our own self-criticism and the damning effect it has on our ability to dream. And then again, we may not be aware. Like an undetected parasite, self-defeatism can long live undetected inside of us, sucking the lifeblood of our dreams. Invasive thoughts can strike at the core of us because they have grown and festered there for quite some time. The point of infection may be traceable to a harsh word or rejection from a person of prominence in our lives. That individual may have inflicted the wound in a brief moment of malice or ignorance, but either way it goes on living inside of us, wreaking havoc in our souls.

I once met an artist who was in her sixties but still carried a wound from a college professor who said her art would never amount to anything. As she recounted the story to me, her eyes welled up. The wound may have been decades old, but it still produced fresh tears.

Dear reader, if you have been carrying a wound like this, you have my utmost sympathy. I write, speak, and pray against this work of evil in your life in no uncertain terms. You need to know that even if self-skepticism has metastasized itself inside of you, it is not a part of you. Fear, doubt, and disbelief are contrivances of the Enemy, which, if implanted in your maker's heart, can hinder your God-given ability to create at its source.

Therefore, defeating the traitorous enemy within is paramount. The first battle waged in the war of creation is silent and unseen and begins at the level of thought. Rooting out the subconscious self-sabotage is difficult to do but must be done in order to restore your ability to dream effectively.

In his book *Orthodoxy*, G. K. Chesterton wrote on the "suicide of thought." He described a kind of overwrought skepticism that can eventually snuff out all matter of generative thinking. He said, "There is a thought that stops thought. That is the only thought that ought to be stopped."[2]

Being skeptical, as I said before, has its time and place, but it takes a fatal turn when criticism turns to cynicism and burrows its way into your heart. Soon, your entire outlook is trained to see only obstacles instead of opportunities. The eventual blunting of your ambition after it is repeatedly run into walls becomes a useless weight to you, and so you toss it aside. You tell yourself it is better not to dream at all than to suffer the "derision for disappointed hopes," to borrow a phrase from Jane Austen.[3]

Upward counterfactual thinking is a poor knockoff of dreaming and another symptom of self-defeatism. Counterfactuals are aimed at the past, which cannot be changed, instead of the future, which can. Upward counterfactuals sound like, "I could have been a great guitarist if only I had practiced more," or "I would have a booming business by now if I had only struck out on my own when I was young." Instead of filling your heart with hope, upward counterfactuals make it sick with its bygone passage. Dreaming, however, keeps you firmly oriented toward the future with no regard for regret. Dreaming says, "I want to be a great guitarist one day, so I am going to start practicing every night," or "I want to own a thriving business one day, so I am going to lay the groundwork now."

ROOTING OUT THE SUBCONSCIOUS SELF-SABOTAGE IS DIFFICULT TO DO BUT MUST BE DONE IN ORDER TO RESTORE YOUR ABILITY TO DREAM EFFECTIVELY.

A Practice in Positivity

Beyond habituating yourself away from the negative, you need to establish practices toward the positive. It is not enough to merely tell yourself not to be overly critical, as you would likely fall victim to the pink elephant paradox: If someone tells you *not* to think of a pink elephant, you think of exactly that. In fact, you are thinking of it now. This is also called the ironic process theory. In a psyche sick with cynicism, harping on yourself for being negative is just one more manifestation of your negativity. You must break the cycle. Every act of creation involves destruction, and the best place to begin is by destroying your negative thoughts.

Flip the script. Take the teeth out of the tiger. See setbacks as opportunities to regroup and innovate. See limitations not as roadblocks to your process but as creative decisions already made for you. An ordinary person can find the silver lining on every cloud, but you are not ordinary. You are functioning at the height of your creativity. Like the farmer invites the rain because billowing clouds make for bountiful crops, you can embrace new challenges knowing they will grow your creative capacity.

EVERY ACT OF CREATION INVOLVES DESTRUCTION, AND THE BEST PLACE TO BEGIN IS BY DESTROYING YOUR NEGATIVE THOUGHTS.

More than just an exercise in optimism, finding joy in the midst of trials is a spiritual discipline (see James 1). Scripture is full of antinomies (seemingly contradictory ideas) such as "Many who are first will be last, and the last first" (Matthew 19:30), "Whoever loses his life for my sake will find it" (Matthew 16:25), and "Whoever exalts himself will be humbled, and whoever humbles himself will be exalted" (Matthew 23:12). It would seem that God flips the script a lot, which is easy for Him to do as the almighty playwright. But it is not the business of God alone to turn the tables; as imitators of God, we are called to do the same. We reflect the Maker's heart in our own when we take a hopeless situation, flip it around, and breathe life into it.

When you have planted that seed of thought, weeded the ground of negativity, and soaked it thoroughly with hope, soon it will break the surface for its first taste of sunlight. The next phase of the maker's process is to begin the critical step of materializing the idea. Sharpen your pencil; it's time to sketch!

CHAPTER FIVE

THE SKETCH

Start Small

When I first started drawing as a kid, I always wondered why the sketches of so-called masters were so scribbly. I figured an accomplished artist would always produce sketches with nice, clean lines, which circumscribed exactly what it was that they wanted to draw. As I grew in my understanding of the function of sketches and my skill in making them, I came to realize that it is a bit of stabbing in the dark (or in this case, the stark whiteness of the page)—a sort of working out of the artist's thoughts. An artist may have a clear image in their head of what they want to create, but translating it from what they know to what they see takes a bit of exploration mixed with experimentation. Oftentimes, aspects I did not consider in my thoughts become evident on the page. In this way, the process of sketching feels like a fluid extension of thinking. It is indeed a continuation of the ideation process taken to the preliminary material stage.

C. S. Lewis once posited to a friend that "the thing he most loved about writing was that it did two things at once. 'I don't know what I mean till I see what I've said.' In other words writing and thinking were a single process."[1]

For Lewis, writing was his opportunity to sketch his thoughts down on paper and thereby perpetuate and massage his ideas. Every maker should establish some version of sketching as the first step of realizing their concepts. It might literally be a sketchbook that you keep close at hand to jot down your thoughts in words or drawings. Or if drawing really isn't your thing, build a mood board in Canva like my wife does when she is redesigning a room in the house. If you are a fiction writer or playwright, try writing a short story or a scene around a character you are trying to develop. Materializing some small aspect of your larger creation and playing around with it is your own sketch and a quick reward of seeing your ideas come to life, which will further spur your creativity.

All too often people tell me about fantastic ideas they have, but they never come to more than that. A kind of creative constipation occurs, and the blockage is almost always here at the turn from thought to material. The roughage of a good sketch can get things moving again. The distance from an idea's first spark to final realization may be a quantum leap that can intimidate the maker from ever getting started. Indeed, that journey is a long one, but it is made little by little. Breaking down the process into incremental steps can take the intimidation out of the task. You can eat the elephant one bite at a time.

The Thumbnail Sketch

A thumbnail sketch is a glimpse on paper; think of it as the sketch of a sketch. When I develop a concept for an art piece, I create not just a single rendering but sequential iterations of sketches that build on one another, and the first is always a thumbnail. As the name implies, the thumbnails are small, quick drawings that take very little time. I can rapidly explore multiple ideas or variations of the same idea in a series of sketches and compare the lot. I'm still miles away from the finished product but I am inching closer, and that is progress enough.

Whatever you make, find the easy way in. Give yourself the most gradual slope to conquer the mountain of creation you are climbing. Prototypes, rough drafts, trials, rehearsals, and dry runs are all versions of the sketch. It is a chance not only to make a start but to refine your approach before you begin in the final creation.

Find every means to take the intimidation out of this step. For me, the less substantial the materials I use during this phase the better. Ironically enough, jotting my ideas on cheaper paper adds to the fluidity of thought. For instance, I would not want to do a sketch on fine watercolor paper or calfskin vellum. Such materials are far too dear for a concept that I might crumple up and throw away. Therefore, the less precious the substrate the better. This is why some of my grandest ideas have been born in pocket

FIND EVERY MEANS TO TAKE THE INTIMIDATION OUT OF THIS STEP.

sketchbooks, on scraps of paper, or on the back of a napkin. When there is nothing precious about the material in front of me, I am not afraid of soiling it with what might be a rubbish idea. This early on, I do not want to be married to any one concept. Zeroing in on the right idea often involves a long process of elimination. Some sketches are drawn just to be ruled out or to get my thoughts flowing. And some rise from the heap to be far more precious than the material they are scribbled on.

An Empire on the Back of a Napkin

I was once commissioned to create a facsimile of a contract written on a restaurant napkin for a billionaire philanthropist. It was written before he had grown his vast portfolio and earned his fortune. I was given the original napkin contract, which had faded quite badly over the forty-some-odd years since it had been written. I had to trace the handwriting on the cloth napkin and match it for the variation of pressure and speed of writing. You can tell a lot about a man when you travel a page in his pen strokes.

ZEROING IN ON THE RIGHT IDEA OFTEN INVOLVES A LONG PROCESS OF ELIMINATION.

I could discern the angst of the moment in the close compression of his letterforms. I could feel his determination in the boldness of his downstrokes, his optimism in the height of his ascenders. It was an odd little job, but the napkin was of great import to the gentleman—indeed, one of his prized keepsakes. He had written the contract for a business deal on the spot with a friend over dinner. As it happened, all his future success would hinge on that small square cloth. That simple linen napkin was all that stood between potential success and absolute ruin for this man at that point in time. No wonder he held on to it for so long and after so many successful business deals since.

I have had some rare relics and exemplars pass through my hands over the years (most of which are far more beautiful than that napkin contract), but the weight of that transcription I will never forget. It was a thumbnail sketch of a business venture that would grow into an empire. That entrepreneurial genius seized the moment without lawyers, board members, or bean counters present, or even a proper piece of paper to draft his contract on. Rather than delay, he acted on a momentary idea with what was immediately at hand. Many great things have very humble beginnings.

Being able to create something out of almost nothing in a moment's notice is a mark of the maker's heart. The imaginative powers at play during these critical moments can lead to monumental breakthroughs. To dare, to wonder, to dream, and *to do* something with all that daring, wondering, and dreaming—no matter how insignificant it might seem—is true bravery. The maker's heart pricked to the possibility of the moment is one of the rare courageous forces in the world, and it can move mountains.

Heaven Meeting Earth

The Cathedral of Santa Maria del Fiore in Florence is one of my favorite pieces of architecture in the world. A feat of human engineering, artistry, and fortitude, it was begun in 1296 and not completed until 1436. The facade of the duomo—arrayed in a triatic color scheme of white Carrara, green Prato serpentine, and red Siena marbles—was added much later and finally finished in 1887.

The footprint is in the shape of a Roman cross with its long nave and three arcades. But the real crown of the cathedral is Filippo Brunelleschi's dome, or *cupola.*

The duomo is one of my architectural favorites because it stands as a spiring testament to the faith of the ones who built it. Yes, it is a house of God, that much is obvious, but what is less obvious is the faith exercised during the course of its creation. The duomo was always intended to be roofed with the spiring dome we see today. But at the time the architectural plans were drawn up, no one knew how to build such a structure. So, you would think new plans would be drawn up and an alternative style of roof would be devised, at least one that they actually knew how to build. But the dome was more than just a stylistic choice; it was intended to mark the very place where heaven meets earth.

Four is the number of humanity. We occupy four dimensions, the fourth being time. The earth in which we dwell is defined by its four directions: north, south, east, and west. There are four legs to a chair, four sides to a house, and four chambers of the human heart. The four-sided structure of the duomo, therefore, symbolizes the earthly realm as it rises out of the ground. Yes, it is far more complicated than a simple box, but it is still composed of straight sides, right angles, and a pronounced geometric interior.

The circle is the symbol of the divine, of eternity. So, whenever you see a round structure on top of a square one in medieval and Renaissance architecture, it is speaking to the convergence of heaven and earth, of God meeting man. When you progress through the nave of the cathedral and come beneath the domed roof with no central supporting structure, your eyes are drawn through a perfectly circular opening toward heaven.

Now you have some understanding of why the roof shape was such an imperative for the duomo's brave architects. Here is where faith entered the equation: Although no one in all Christendom knew how to build such a structure, the builders believed that at the appointed time, when the base of the cathedral was finished, God would bring someone who possessed the wisdom to know how to create the dome.

Building a cathedral is a generations-long endeavor. Families by and large stuck to the trade they were in, and knowledge would pass from father to son. Many of the stonemasons who laid the final blocks of the marble on the duomo could look down at its base and see the handiwork of their grandfather or even great-grandfather. It could very well be that at the time the cornerstone for the cathedral was laid, the architect for the roof was yet to be born. And so it was with the Santa Maria del Fiore.

In fact, the gaping circular hole in the duomo's roof sat open to the elements for fifty-six years waiting for the right architect to come along.

Enter Brunelleschi. This unconventional craftsman with a fiery temper once got himself thrown out of a public gathering for claiming he would erect the cupola without any central supporting structure. Brunelleschi was a genius and mastered pretty much anything he put his hands to. He was a sculptor, goldsmith, and clockmaker before he was eventually regarded as maybe the world's first *real* architect.

Italy during the Renaissance was a highly competitive atmosphere. Long before it was unified as a country in 1861, Italy was fragmented into states, duchies, and kingdoms that were in constant competition and occasionally at war with each other. Add to it that the powers that be within the warring states held contests for pretty much every major commission, innovation, and building project. Competition was the crucible that refined and galvanized the very best available talent during this exciting time in history.

And the financiers, politicians, and church leaders certainly knew how to turn up the heat.

The competition for the builder of the cupola was a long and ongoing one, with many throwing their hats in the ring. Audacious plans of great complexity were presented before the committee. Yet Brunelleschi took another approach. He challenged the judges to stand a chicken's egg on its end. After each of the judges failed, Brunelleschi showed them how. He simply cracked the egg in half and—*presto!*—a perfect dome was standing. Brunelleschi won the competition by impressing them with the fact that even the most complex problem can be solved by looking at it in the simplest way.

The chicken's egg was Brunelleschi's sketch, and barely a thumbnail at best. The cupola in the end was a massively complex structure—a dome within a dome, for he built it in two layers of spiraling, fishbone-patterned masonry. But like a chicken's egg, all exterior pressure is distributed evenly across the *spina di pesce* (herringbone), so his "sketch" was accurate even in its simplicity. It took him sixteen years of grueling work with critics constantly looking over his shoulder, but it remains to this day the largest masonry dome in the world, and proof that the grandest ideas can be hatched from the smallest eggs!

So start small. Start now. Get into the habit of jotting down your ideas, no matter how trivial you might think them. Establish a method of sketching respective to the kind of maker that you are. It may be on the back of a napkin or a chicken egg or something else entirely, so long as you take that first critical step toward realizing your thoughts. Soon enough, you will be thinking with a pencil in hand and

THE GRANDEST IDEAS CAN BE HATCHED FROM THE SMALLEST EGGS!

then burning up both ends of lead and eraser in a furious exercise of imaginative discovery. When at length dreaming and drawing coalesce, you are ready to begin building the *armature* for what that sketch has revealed.

CHAPTER SIX

ARMATURE

The Supportive Structure

Whenever I model in clay, I begin by building the armature. Think of it as the skeleton of the sculpture. The armature is usually twisted aluminum wire of various thicknesses depending on the size of the sculpture. When forming a figure, for instance, I would begin by building a simple stick figure out of wire and positioning it in the desired pose. At this point my statuette looks not much different than one of my kids' pipe-cleaner crafts. As rudimentary as it might appear, the armature is critical to the future development and lasting success of the art piece.

Once the armature is established, I can start layering the clay over the top of it. My understructure serves auxiliary purposes besides structural support. For one thing, it defines the general proportions of the figure. By the definitive kinks in the wire, I establish where the joints of the limbs are. The armature also helps me find the overall expression of the sculpture before I build up the clay. If I can imbue the simple wire stick man with life through the dynamism of the pose, then I know I am on the right track. I do not want to rely on the final details alone to animate my statue—life has to come from within. Sculptors who rush the armature and rely too much on the final layers of skin and clothing to animate their figures end up creating statues that look static and rigid. Worse than that, their figures can lose proper proportion and have distorted anatomy if their skeletal structure is not in place.

No matter what you are making, you should always begin by establishing armature. Every house needs studs and a foundation; every business needs a business plan; every story needs a plot; every sermon needs an outline; every song needs a melody. The armature may be as tangible as the steel girders holding up the Statue of Liberty, or as visceral as the ideals upheld in the Constitution of the United States.

The armature phase is maybe not the most enjoyable part of the creation process, but it is foundational to the future success of whatever you are building. Furthermore, it makes the rest of the journey all the more clear. You can continue to grow your project, business, enterprise, or craft with greater confidence once you know you are set on the right path. Slowness is a drum I will continue to beat throughout this book, and it certainly applies here. You would not want to rush through the armature process or skip it altogether just because you are anxious to get to the fun stuff. Remember, slow progress is lasting progress. The time spent on this less-exciting stage is far less regrettable than discovering too late how foundational it is.

Shortcuts and Long-Suffering

Leonardo da Vinci was an innovator of historic proportions. But our greatest strength can become our greatest weakness where it is misapplied, and such was the case for Leonardo's murals.

REMEMBER, SLOW PROGRESS IS LASTING PROGRESS.

Fresco murals were very popular during the High Renaissance. As the name of that era suggests, frescoes, like many other motifs of art and design, were reborn from antiquity. The process by which frescoes are painted was well established long before Leonardo ever picked up a paintbrush. Wet plaster is applied to the wall. Before it is given a chance to dry, the artist paints onto the plaster while it is still fresh—hence, fresco. The wet plaster and the paint pigments form a very solid bond as they both cure together on the wall or ceiling. A good fresco true to form can last for millennia. The oldest known fresco dates to between 3500 and 3200 BC.

Creating a fresco requires a lot of time and careful coordination. Many people imagine that when Michelangelo painted the Sistine Chapel ceiling, he was working alone. While I am sure Michelangelo would have preferred to work alone, the fresco process does not allow for it. He was likely working with a fairly large team of fellow artisans and craftspeople. He might have been the only one wielding the artist's brush, but he was just the last stage of a carefully choreographed sequence.

First, you would have had a couple of people mixing the plaster according to Michelangelo's exact specifications. That would then be hoisted up the scaffolding to a second team at the top that would carefully apply it. The plaster must be smooth, of even thickness, and applied only in the area the artist was ready to paint. The third stage would involve a team taking the sketches that the artist had prepared on large sheets of paper, which would have been perforated along its outline using needles. Once the sketch was held in place against the wet plaster, someone would pounce charcoal dust through the perforated holes, thereby transferring the artist's sketch into the plaster. Finally, the artist would begin furiously painting before the plaster dried.

Ever being one to defy convention, Leonardo took it on himself to find a way of painting murals that was far less laborious than the traditional fresco method. He actually experimented with a couple of different methods. Tragically, many of his murals started falling off the walls he had painted them on during his lifetime. His mural *The Last Supper*, in Milan, Italy, is the greatest surviving mural from Leonardo, and it is very fragile.

If you want to view *The Last Supper* today, you have to book tickets way in advance. Only a very limited number of visitors are allowed each year owing to the fact that the mural must be carefully protected. The painting and the room it is housed in have been completely sealed off from the outer environment. If you are lucky enough to book tickets, you have to sit in a room adjacent to the mural for an extended period of time while the air temperature and humidity are equalized with that of the mural's chamber. Simultaneously, any pollutants that may have come in with the visitors are scrubbed from the air using a network of filters.

The temperature, humidity, and cleanliness of the air surrounding the mural are rigorously controlled in an effort to slow the deterioration process. A team of art restorers monitors the mural closely and constantly, and they are always working to stabilize it.

On our honeymoon, Hannah and I, not knowing the rigors of the visiting process, were unable to secure tickets to see Leonardo's crumbling masterpiece. As we were wandering through the streets of Milan, we stumbled upon an antique bookshop. Once inside, we marveled at the realization that what the Italians refer to as antique is far different from our American notion of the same idea. Verily, there were books on the shelves, several in fact, that were older than the United States.

A woven cane rack at the end of one of the shelves held some art prints. I thumbed through the stack and discovered they were all original, very old copperplate engravings. Many of them were of quaint Tuscan countryside scenes. At length, I flipped to somewhere in the middle of the stack, and lo and behold, there was an engraving after Leonardo's *The Last Supper* mural—the one we were not able to see! It was as if the light of heaven was emanating from that art piece in the rack, washing my face in a glorious sheen of radiant light like some scene out of an Indiana Jones film. Here was my holy grail! I swore I could hear angels harmonizing a heavenly tune around me. I scraped together the last of our travel budget (and then some) and bought the piece. It was the most expensive work of art I had purchased at the time, but I would not leave Italy without it. All the way home, I felt like I was smuggling some ancient artwork out of the country, and so I was. I got over it pretty quickly. Italy still has a lot of art left, as it turns out!

Originally engraved in 1787, *The Last Supper* is beautifully framed and hangs in our master bedroom above a carved oak secretary's desk. The engraver, or *sculpsit* as they are called, would have been studying a version of Leonardo's mural that was more intact than it is today. I love that piece. I love it not only for its iconic beauty or as the greatest souvenir of our honeymoon or for how it helped redeem a missed opportunity. But as I look at it and think of the mural which is its prototype and the way I know it is ever crumbling from the wall, it's as if I hear Leonardo whisper to me, "*Do not forsake what is foundational.*"

Innovation is not in itself a bad thing. But if you are going to break with convention and go your own way, then you better know what you are giving up. Historical precedent can work as a kind of armature to undergird a new innovation's forward growth. Having a time-tested method at your disposal enables you to build with greater confidence.

Plan Your Work

One of the greatest gifts I have ever received was the opportunity to do a LifePlan and StratOp with none other than Pete Richardson, the cofounder of the Paterson Group.

Pete Richardson, alongside his mentor Tom Paterson, formulated the LifePlan and StratOp process to help people structure their lives, businesses, and organizations around their core purpose. The process is not so much a reinvention as a revelation and realignment to what is inside of you. The aim of their method is to help you define what is central to your calling and plan your future actions accordingly. For anyone who is longing for this kind of in-depth guidance either personally or professionally (or both), I highly recommend it.

Hannah and I did our LifePlan together, which is a common approach for couples through the Paterson process. The morning of, our LifePlan arrived, and we made the scenic drive along the Front Range to the Richardsons' home in northwestern Colorado. Pete greeted us on the charming wraparound porch of his historic home, made all the lovelier by the stylings of his beloved wife, Janet. Pete and Janet have become like family to us. So, stepping through their threshold always feels like coming home. After a nice catch-up in the kitchen with the Richardsons, Pete ushered us down to their subfloor basement. With earthenware mugs full of fresh coffee and notebooks in hand, we made our descent. Behind a solid wood arched door is the room where it happens.

Stepping into Pete's "war room," as he calls it, set the tone for the kind of lasting foundational work we would undergo. Old wood paneling and reclaimed wood beams articulate the ceiling. The walls are of rough stone tightly tessellated with a small fireplace in the center back wall. On the opposite wall are large glass panels that run the full height and length. To the far left of the panels is a walnut rocking chair, handcrafted in the signature Sam Maloof style. If I knew nothing else about Pete, I could look at his chair and know he is a man of surpassing wisdom and good taste.

In the center of the room facing the glass panels are two leather chairs with a small hand-carved table in the middle. These were for us—we were given front-row seats to the story of our lives' purpose.

We settled in for the two-day intensive—my wife and I in our armchairs and Pete in his rocker. He opened our session in prayer and read a short verse out of his well-worn Bible to frame our time together. "The heart of man plans his way, but the LORD establishes his steps" (Proverbs 16:9). Pete's voice always reminds me of Jeff Bridges's. He has that kind of iconic tone when he speaks that makes you want to stop what you are doing and lean in. Whenever he says something profound, his volume gets a little lower and the texture of his voice becomes slightly more gruff. The man is a deep well of wisdom, and you want to catch every life-giving drop that falls from his lips.

At length, Pete popped the cap off his dry-erase marker, and we were off to the races! Utilizing the glass panels and a large pad of flip chart paper, Pete led us on an exploratory journey of our own values, purposes, dreams, and ambitions. He has led more than a thousand people through LifePlans over the years, and it was fun to see the master at work. He steered us through the Paterson method, and he filled page after giant page with the unfolding narrative of our lives.

Probing questions that built on one another revealed so much more than we had imagined. His hand moved furiously to capture our every word as they bubbled up in response to his stirring queries. After each page was filled, he tore it from that pad and hung it up around the room. By the end of our time together, we were surrounded by our LifePlan, exploded on every wall and written in Pete's own hand. By the end of day two, we rose from our armchairs, mentally and emotionally spent but so heartened by the journey we had been on. We took a moment to look around the room and soak it all in. In two days we had formed a vision and mission statement for our lives; identified our core values; established replenishment cycles; made one-, five-, and ten-year goals; and so much more besides.

A few months later Pete had us back to do a StratOp for our businesses, which involved a very similar process but with a more entrepreneurial slant.

As Pete said at the outset, planning is a way that we faithfully step into the things God has called us to, but He ultimately establishes our steps. There is a tension that exists between planning our lives and surrendering to God's will. If you are planning in the right way, however, then understanding God's will for your life is exactly what you are looking for in planning.

I know how rare and special it is to have an opportunity like this with the man who guided us, and we do not take that for granted. Thank you, Pete! You may not have the time, resources, or relationship to allow for something like a formal LifePlan, but I would still encourage you to plan with intentionality for your life and your business if that is something that applies to you. Yes, "the heart of man plans his way"; that heart is a maker's heart, and that plan is the armature which undergirds your work. If we want our lives to be modeled on and supported by God's purpose for us, then we need to take the time to identify exactly what that is.

"Unless the LORD builds the house, those who build it labor in vain" (Psalm 127:1). Too often people do not bother to inquire of the Lord as to a plan for their life. Many more do not bother to plan at all. Without a guiding ethos to hold you to your calling, you are destined to live a nebulous existence. You may be a diligent worker and passionate about what you do, but if you lack the language and understanding of your purpose, then it is easy for outside influences to determine your destiny for you.

IF WE WANT OUR LIVES TO BE MODELED ON AND SUPPORTED BY GOD'S PURPOSE FOR US, THEN WE NEED TO TAKE THE TIME TO IDENTIFY EXACTLY WHAT THAT IS.

I am an artist, but I realized a long time ago that art is not the only thing I make. I am a *working artist*, which means I have created a business as well. If I strive so tirelessly to build the necessary armature into my art pieces to ensure their structural integrity, then why on earth would I not do the same for my business, through which all my art is created and sold? It would not make sense. I want to approach all my creations with the same level of intentionality and care.

Pete says, "If you plan your work and work your plan, then your plan will work." It is not good enough to merely make a plan without executing it; that would be foolishness. As I type away this evening, I am currently *working my plan*. One of the very things that we discussed in the StratOp for my business was the opportunity to write books. We took the idea through a decision-making exercise to ensure it aligned with my mission and the core values of my business. You cannot be too surprised to learn that it passed! Writing books aligned greatly with my calling to teach as well as create. But other things did not pass muster. Things I was already doing and had been doing for quite some time. Into the same decision-making formula they went but did not come out on the other side. I am no longer doing those things.

If I were to deviate from my armature and start adding on wild extensions of clay where there was no support, it would be bound to crumble and I would have built in vain. Armature, therefore, works as a sort of accountability system, keeping you honest to what is central to you. It makes saying no to the wrong things just as clear as saying yes to the things that align with your core.

Building the armature may be one of the unfun fundamentals of making, but you understand its value now. Take the time to get it right, and the rest will follow easily. Your work will be a sound structure; it will be imbued with life from its core. It will have the integrity to last through the ages because you have not forsaken what is foundational. So ready your maker's heart; it is time to gather your tools for making!

CHAPTER SEVEN

TOOLS OF THE TRADE

Calling Your Soldiers to Battle

As an artist who works in multiple mediums, I need a wide array of tools—at least that is the official story I tell my wife and my bookkeeper. I have tools for drawing, tools for painting, and tools for sculpting. I even have tools to maintain my tools, like sharpening systems, specialty cleaners, and organizers. Many of those tools, especially my calligraphy pens, I have made myself. What is the right number of tools for one man to have? Why, all of them, of course!

I have not amassed a plethora of tools for mere collecting's sake.

To me, they are like Rumpelstiltskin's magical loom, and with them I can turn straw into gold. Give me a well-tuned writing instrument and I can make music on the page. A quality paintbrush becomes a magic wand in my hands, and where I wave it, new and wonderful things appear. With a push and a twist, my engraving tool becomes a golden key that unlocks a world of beauty. And my racks of carving chisels are like a brigade of soldiers, standing ready to go into creative battle, and they wait only for my command.

You may have ascertained already from my waxing poetic about tools that I am passionate about the role they play in the act of making. I was itching to write this chapter. I love to talk shop and to tinker. The technical aspect of my work is one of the things that inspires and invigorates me. Moreover, I think it is an important practical facet of creating that is too often overlooked for the theoretical. The right tool can draw you into a creative mindset, make your process easier, increase your effectiveness, and call out the best in you. Conversely, the wrong tool can obstruct your creativity, frustrate your efforts, and limit your potential. Even more than that, it can be downright dangerous.

> THE RIGHT TOOL CAN DRAW YOU INTO A CREATIVE MINDSET, MAKE YOUR PROCESS EASIER, INCREASE YOUR EFFECTIVENESS, AND CALL OUT THE BEST IN YOU.

Quality Matters

My first major woodcarving project was a carousel-style rocking horse I made in high school woodshop. While most kids were making cutting boards or little jewelry boxes, I took it upon myself to design and carve a rocking horse—complete with a spiraling brass pole and five-foot maple rockers. I had taken the time in some of my off periods before woodshop to draw up the plans for my rocking stallion on a graph paper pad. When I presented my woodshop teacher with the drafting plans, he told me it was very ambitious, but he had seen my other artwork and thought I was fit for the task.

Up to that point, my only other carving experience was whittling in the woods, and this was going to require more than my pocketknife. To do any serious carving, you really need a library of quality carving chisels, as I have now in my shop. But as a broke high school kid, I could not afford the investment of a good set of gouges at fifty dollars a pop. So I scoured eBay to find something that would fit within my very limited budget. I ended up buying some cheap carving set with "Made in China" proudly stamped in the splintery wood handles. It arrived in an awful plastic wrap sheath and soaked in machining oil to keep the low-grade steel from rusting in the package. I tried them out on the block form of the horse I had cut out on the shop class bandsaw, but they were dull as a spoon. Even if I had known at the time how to properly sharpen a chisel (which I didn't), I doubt they would have even held an edge. I remember thinking the horse would take forever to carve if I went this route. Back to eBay to do some more shopping.

I ended up finding a four-inch-diameter carving head that attached to an angle grinder. It had teeth to a chainsaw on it and when attached to a grinder would spin at 1,100 rpm. This was certainly going to speed things up! The tool was aptly named The Lance-a-Lot. I smashed the "Buy It Now" button.

The only thing I needed after that was the grinder to put it on. So I found the cheapest generic angle grinder eBay had to offer and bought that too.

My new carving setup was everything I was hoping for. It chewed through the basswood and sprayed a shower of sawdust from its razor-sharp teeth. It was loud and wickedly dangerous. Inside the vent slots of the grinder, I would occasionally see sparks flash. If I ran it too long, it would get hot in my hands and give off a terrible electric smell. But I didn't let any of that faze me. I was making good progress, and I eventually got a handle on that gyrating, sparking, wood-eating beast.

After just a couple of weeks of use, the on-and-off switch on the grinder broke. When I turned the switch off, the grinder just kept running. So I stepped on the end of the extension cord it was plugged into and yanked out the plug of the grinder. At this point, a smarter person would have at least thrown out the broken grinder and bought another one of greater quality. In hindsight, I should have taken it as a bad omen that the machine was rising up against me and I would have been better off burying it in a deep hole somewhere far away. But nope! I kept using that janky carving contraption from eBay hell even in its broken and rebellious state. Every time I wanted to use it, I would set it on the workbench and *plug 'er in and let 'er rip*! And when I wanted to turn it off, I would repeat my stomp-and-yank maneuver.

One day after school I decided to stay and work on my horse in the woodshop. I was getting very close to finishing and was excited with how it had taken shape. With Lance-a-Lot mounted on his unbridled and drunken mule of a grinder, I got to work. As I often did, I stepped back from the piece a bit to observe the overall shape. I would tilt my head this way and that as I studied the horse and noted where else I needed to take off some more wood. Meanwhile, I was still holding the screaming grinder in my hand.

To this day, I cannot recall exactly how, but in an instant the index finger on my left hand met the fury of the whirling, toothed blade. I yanked my hand back and looked immediately down at my finger in horror. In a fraction of a second, those chainsaw teeth had ripped off my fingernail, mangled my flesh, and, I would later learn through X-rays, shaved off a small piece of my bone. I stomped and yanked that stupid plug for the very last time and threw the grinder on the bench. I rushed over to the paper towel dispenser on the far side of the room, muttering choice words the whole way. Racking the feeder lever several times in a fit of panic, I tore the thin brown paper towel from its perforating teeth. I bunched it up around the end of my bloody, lacerated finger and squeezed tight.

An hour or so later, I was lying inside an overcrowded emergency room on a gurney, owing to my lightheadedness, while still holding my finger. While I lay there staring at the ceiling tiles awaiting my turn to see a doctor, I was filled with a kind of buyer's remorse I had never known before . . . or since.

I share this rather gruesome story with you to emphasize an important point about tools: Quality matters! And I declare that with my stubby left index finger raised high in the air . . . though a little less high than it otherwise would be had the grinder not *lanced-my-finger-a-lot*!

Tool Connoisseur

I have grown a great deal since that fateful day in my high school woodshop. I am now a very discerning shopper of quality tools. *Buy nice or buy twice* is my philosophy! I can smell a poorly made device from a mile away. When shopping out a new piece of equipment to add to my lineup, I will invest a lot of time researching and reading customer reviews. That process also affords me the opportunity to think through my execution on a more granular level. I think through my approach and what tools I will use at various stages of the process and how. If I can, I like to get my hands on a particular contrivance before I make my purchase and maybe even put it through its paces. Most of the time, I can discern the craftsmanship or lack thereof with a simple once-over in person. Often, I can tell if a utensil is up to snuff or not merely by looking at the pictures online. I might see a listing of a pen and think the manufacturer totally messed up the ergonomics of its grip, or I might see a backbent gouge and think it is too doglegged to carve gracefully. You are right if you think this information is completely obscure to the average person, but to me it is an integral part of mastering my craft. I know my tools, and I know what I demand of them.

Consider the tools in your own respective area of mastery. How might the acquisition, utilization, and deeper understanding of your instruments elevate your craft and calling? Do the tools you have now draw you into your work or struggle against you? There will always be external resistance to the creative process that we cannot control, whereas internal resistance can be greatly reduced simply by choosing the right tools and materials. Nothing is more frustrating than being impeded by the very things that were meant to aid you in your work. I take pleasure in banishing into the eternal darkness of a trash can a tool that does not perform as it should or a pen that does not write properly. And as I chuck them into the bin, I declare, "Away from me, you wicked servant!"

Romancing the Tool

Elevate your instruments beyond mere practicality into the realm of romanticism. I not only make my calligraphy pens to feel good in the hand but also use fine materials and carve them with ornate details, which heightens my affinity for them.

Tools tell a story, and you can add to that story. I once used my great-grandfather's depth gauge to help make the mortise and tenon joinery on the base of our baby's swan cradle. My attention to the task at hand was centered on the fact that I was connecting generations of my family in an act of craftsmanship. A good friend of ours and accomplished author uses a Bluetooth keyboard that looks and sounds like an antique type-writer. The click and clack of the keys draws her into the rhythm of writing. I have since bought a similar keyboard myself and am joyfully clacking away on it now!

DO THE TOOLS YOU HAVE NOW DRAW YOU INTO YOUR WORK OR STRUGGLE AGAINST YOU?

Fit for the Task

A professional chef needs well-balanced knives that can hold a good edge for the thousands of critical cuts in a single night of service. They need good pans that evenly conduct heat to achieve the perfect sauté. An ultramarathon runner takes account of every fraction of an ounce in their shoes, as the cumulative strides of the runner multiply those ounces into hundreds of pounds moved by their legs during a race. Yo-Yo Ma performs with a 1712 Davidov Stradivarius because the quality of that instrument is matched to the rarity of his acquired skill and talent.

I would even expand the definition of tools to include space. For if you are a practitioner in the realms of hospitality, teaching, counseling, or the performing arts, space becomes a tool of your craft. In the art of hospitality, your home is an extension of yourself as you wrap arms around all those who enter in. Space can be arranged to better inspire, comfort, instruct, or entertain. A performer commands the stage the same way I do a paintbrush and yearns for it similarly as well.

Tools Do Not the Master Make

While I did say at the start of this chapter in no uncertain terms that I desire *all* the tools, perhaps that was a little tongue-in-cheek. There are times when less is more. I still want the highest quality of whatever I use, but too many tools can bog down the process. I happen to be very technically minded, but I have come to realize that not everyone is that way.

My wife, Hannah, is a wonderful photographer. She takes all the product shots of the art and jewelry for our websites. For a long time, she was setting up near our bedroom window because that is where she got the best light. I found her one day taking pictures of some jewelry pieces on a swatch of canvas sprawled out on the floor of our bedroom while balancing a nylon diffuser between the carpet and her head. She was freehanding her shots with a macro lens, which if you understand anything about photography, you know that is very hard to do.

After observing Hannah in her makeshift state, the tool nerd in me jumped into action. I went on a research binge and shopping spree for the best photography setup to suit her every need. I bought her a top-of-the-line temperature-controlled LED light—complete with multiple filters. I bought tripods, diffusers, reflectors, and a special product photography table with an infinity backdrop. I got it all set up for her and walked her through every knob, apparatus, and feature. She was genuinely grateful and at that time very excited to use it.

About a week went by and I ran up to our room to grab something. There I found Hannah with her same ramshackle setup as before. I asked her why she wasn't using the veritable photography studio I had assembled for her in the basement. She shrugged her shoulders and simply replied, "This is easier."

While I would still encourage you to use the very best of tools at your disposal, this word of advice comes with a couple of caveats. First, you have to define what is *best for you.* The best tools for you may not mean the best tools in the world or the most tools. There does come a point of diminishing returns, especially in the area of technology, where there is such a broad spectrum of price and features. Hannah uses an entry-level digital SLR camera with a decent quality lens for our product shots, and that works great for her. Most of the time she is not even using that. For our social media pages she is just shooting one-handed on her iPhone with a baby on her hip. Try that, Ansel Adams!

Second, don't let not having the ideal tool stop you from creating. I may enjoy a wide array of tools now as a professional artist, but I certainly did not start out that way. It has taken me a long time and years of investment to build up to what I have now. There are still some pieces that we sell prints of in my online gallery that were done on my childhood drafting table while still living with my parents after college. *Eesh!* I know what it is like to not have access to or not be able to afford the equipment I want. Even now there are tools on my dream list that I cannot justify paying for at the moment. *All* the right tools are not necessary for producing lasting creations, nor are they the guarantor of mastery. Even if you don't have the best tools, you can aim to get the best out of whatever you do have.

Creative Confinement

Several years ago, through a ministry my brother started, our family got connected to a prisoner in the Texas State Penitentiary. His name is Rudolfo, and we affectionately call him "Rudy." Rudy went to prison for robbing several gas stations with a paintbrush. He disguised the paintbrush by wrapping it in a pair of boxer shorts to make it look like a gun. He was eventually caught for his crimes, and the Texas judge who heard the case came down harshly on Rudy and sentenced him to thirty years behind bars.

ALL THE RIGHT TOOLS ARE NOT NECESSARY FOR PRODUCING LASTING CREATIONS, NOR ARE THEY THE GUARANTOR OF MASTERY.

After being incarcerated, Rudy joined a notorious prison gang and rose quickly through the ranks. It was originally a means to his survival. If you can't beat 'em, join 'em. But God soon grabbed hold of his heart. The small prison-issue radio he was given picked up only one channel in his cell at that end of the block—Christian radio. He admits it would not have been his first choice, but it was better than static, so it really was his only choice. The music and messages delivered to his cell each day via that singular airstream began to soften his criminal heart, and he eventually gave his life to Christ.

Rudy knew he had to leave the prison gang, but there was only one way in and one way out. So, after disavowing his allegiance, he had to be put into solitary confinement for his own protection.

Rudy is an artist. You might have guessed this at the beginning of the story when he was using a paintbrush to hold up convenience stores. I will state again, our greatest weakness is our greatest strength misapplied. And Rudy's misapplied paintbrush meant thirty years in the clink. When Rudy wanted to draw or paint in prison, he was limited to the few necessities he could purchase through the commissary. So, he learned to draw with the few tools available to him. He would send our family some of his illustrated calligraphy pieces he had done entirely with a ballpoint pen. His detail and shading were truly phenomenal.

Once he sent my kid sisters handkerchiefs with scenes of Winnie-the-Pooh painted on them. They were beautifully colored and looked like they had been airbrushed. But when we read the accompanying letter Rudy had sent with them, we learned of his ingenious and rather unconventional method. Using a little water to reconstitute the candy-coated shells of M&M's, Rudy flicked the food coloring from the bristles of a toothbrush onto the handkerchiefs. He would use scraps of cardboard to mask off sections where he didn't want the paint to fall. Realizing the hours of tedium involved, we were all the more impressed. I doubt a portrait of Pooh has ever been painted so *sweetly*.

Our entire family's relationship with Rudy grew over the years. My dad mentored Rudy and helped him get his GED. My parents were even able to go down and visit him a couple of times while he was still incarcerated. Rudy was always filled with so much joy, and his letters and art pieces shone with it. He was released early, having served seventeen years of his thirty-year sentence, and now lives with his wife in Texas. He is family to us, and my parents were honored guests at his wedding. He calls them Mom and Dad, and I call him brother.

My mom still has every single one of the many art pieces he so generously sent to us. For a long time, I modeled my handwriting after Rudy's because it was so beautiful and elaborate. It is funny to think that through the Master Penman program, my last mentor was the calligrapher in the White House. But let it be known that my very first mentor was a calligrapher in *the big house.*

Rudy will always be a hero of mine for the skill and ingenuity of his craft and the way he never let his light go out even when he was in the darkest place. There have been many points in my life when I wish I had more or better tools to work with, and that is when I think of Rudy. I have a paint cabinet in our basement where I keep my tubes of museum-quality oil paints. I have every color, hue, and shade you can imagine. In that same cabinet I have a panoply of fine brushes in every size, neatly organized and filling several drawers. As a small reminder to be grateful for what I have and to get the most out of it, in the corner of one drawer I keep a pack of M&M's and a toothbrush.

Whatever tools you have, be grateful for them and strive to get the most out of them. Throughout Scripture, there are a smattering of examples of God using people with the simple tools they already possessed and working mightily through them. For David it was his sling (1 Samuel 17), for Moses it was his staff (Exodus 4; 14), for Samson it was a jawbone of a donkey (Judges 15:15), and for Peter it was his fishing boat (Luke 5:3–6). God may have used nothing more than His voice to speak the universe into existence, but Jesus redeemed the world as the final act of its creation using the least covetable tool of all—the cross.

The Most Important Tools

The most important tools you have are your body, mind, and heart. While these are the most important, I often see makers neglecting or abusing these tools the most.

It seems contradictory for someone to invest a great deal of love, care, and money into their tools but neglect their own faculties, though it happens. And while you can always go out and buy a new machine if it breaks down, you've got only one you. Developing some good habits of self-care is more than just pampering; it is keeping your primary utensils in top working condition to produce the very highest-quality product. Just as maintaining your possessions is an act of good stewardship, how much more critical is it to steward the few assets that are more valuable than all the rest combined and the ones you did not buy but were given to you?

Body

Let me just step aside and share one of the coolest aspects of writing this book. It would seem as though God is ensuring that I practice what I preach *while I am preaching it.* Multiple times while writing this manuscript, I have been in a position of particular poignancy relevant to the very topic I am writing on in the moment. Currently, I am on our stationary bike in our unfinished basement writing this portion on maintenance of the body as a tool. Being the active person that I am, I grew tired of sitting at my computer desk for hours on end while writing this book, so I devised a little makeshift platform on the handlebars of our stationary bike for my laptop to sit on. So here I am, cranking the gears with my feet to match

> THE MOST IMPORTANT TOOLS YOU HAVE ARE YOUR BODY, MIND, AND HEART. WHILE THESE ARE THE MOST IMPORTANT, I OFTEN SEE MAKERS NEGLECTING OR ABUSING THESE TOOLS THE MOST.

with speed the ones in my head, all the while typing through literal sweat on my keyboard to maintain one of my most important tools.

Physical fitness has almost always been a very important part of my life, though I was never a natural athlete. Adolescence for me brought with it a healthy amount of chub. Some of my so-called friends at the time made fun of me, and I became deeply insecure about my body. So I turned to weightlifting to transform my husky physique.

My dad worked out religiously in our basement every morning with a small bench, a treadmill, and some ramshackle weights. He was a natural athlete and had been successful in sports all his life. He was not svelte but bulky, as you would expect a former offensive lineman to be. He had massive arms and a barrel chest, and I always admired him for it.

So I took my turn working out in the basement to try to overcome the "fat kid" stigma that had been assigned to me by my peers. At length, I started gaining muscle and reshaping my generous boyish figure. I graduated out of the basement and into the high school gym my freshman year and worked out faithfully three days a week till I graduated.

In college I got into all-natural bodybuilding, which culminated in a single competition at Muscle Beach in Venice. Once was enough. I didn't care to ever be in front of so many people with so little clothing again. But it was a rite of passage for me that I am grateful to have gone through. College was one of the rare times in my life that I was able to diet and train as hard as I did. It helped me gain mastery over my body and grew my love for fitness.

I still work out today, though not as regularly as I would like being the father of four young kids. But on the whole, I am fairly consistent. I am far from competition shape, but my goals these days are keeping up with my kids, fighting the dad bod, and doing my best to make the missus happy.

Beyond that, I recognize the importance fitness plays in the execution of my work. Some crafts are less physically demanding than others, but all benefit when I am healthy and feeling fit. For instance, you would not think that penmanship, with all the action happening right at my fingertips, would rely so heavily on the rest of my body. However, every part of this human machine is playing some role in what comes out on the page. Only the smallest assisting actions are coming through my fingers. I write using muscular movement, which is movement from the wrist. This allows me to write longer without fatigue and gives greater consistency to my pen strokes. On larger letters and flourishes I use whole-arm movement, which comes clear up from my shoulder and pectoral muscles. I cannot be hunched over my writing desk, supporting myself with my writing arm, because I need it to move freely. My whole torso then must function as a kind of self-stabilizing framework to keep my body erect in the chair and my shoulders suspended and steady while leaning in from the hips, which also involves my core and back muscles. But it doesn't stop there. Where my feet are determines how my weight is shifted in the chair. I cannot have them crossed or bent beneath me. My feet should be firmly planted flat on the floor, and that grounding, in effect, helps stabilize my whole body in the act of writing.

Painting has its own demands, with hours on end standing at the easel. And carving, more than the rest, requires much strength and stamina. Taking care of my body, then, is paramount to my success as a maker. Yes, there have been times when I have pushed my body beyond what I

TAKING CARE OF MY BODY, THEN, IS PARAMOUNT TO MY SUCCESS AS A MAKER.

should have, and my work suffers for it. I want to be creating art for as long as the good Lord allows me, so I need to do my utmost to steward well the instrument He gave me.

Mind

I have a great mother who was vigilant about capturing me in my innocence as a child and guarding my mind carefully. Growing up, she used to use a phrase common to many moms back then: "Garbage in, garbage out." If a show came on TV that she deemed unsuitable, she would walk over to our '80s television set with its bunny-ears antenna and bubbled glass and turn it off while reciting her mantra: "Garbage in, garbage out!" That phrase and the hard boundaries that came with it used to annoy me as a kid, but as an adult and parent now, I so appreciate the guardian she was over my developing mind.

When I was about eight years old, I went over to my good friend Josh's house to play. Generally, all boys at that age love playing "army man," but Josh was prolific at it. He had more toy guns, G.I. Joes, and camouflage than all my other friends combined. Getting a playdate with Josh meant being called up for the draft into his monomaniacal imagination. On this particular day, after hours of gunfights and make-believe explosions, I suggested we draw together for a while if only for the sake of variety. But to appeal to Josh's particular passions, I suggested that we draw some army propaganda posters, though I did not know they were called that at the time. I borrowed a phrase from a patch I had seen on one of Josh's army outfits: "Those who fight with the best, die like the rest!" I drew a big machete in the middle of the phrase with blood running down the blade. Josh thought it was very cool!

At length, my mom came to pick me up after my tour of duty at Josh's house. As I got in our family van, I immediately showed my mom what I had drawn. Ever being one to gush, she always met each drawing I showed her with enthusiasm and praise. This was different. After taking a moment to read my magic marker propaganda poster, she gripped the top of the sheet in her fingertips with both hands, tore it right down the middle, and repeatedly tore it till it was reduced to a stack of small pieces. She turned around, handed me back the shards of paper, looked me squarely in the eyes, and said, "I never want to see you use your gift of drawing like this again." And then she had me go back into Josh's house and apologize to his mother for what I drew. That is the one and only drawing that my mom has ever torn up, and to this day I am thankful she did so.

In this short story from my childhood, you have two examples of making: On the one hand, you have me as a boy exploring the application of my talent and the immediate effect of the input on the output—*garbage in, garbage out.*

On the other hand, you have my mom establishing her household through the protection, correction, and cultivation of her child's mind. And it was not as if my mom was opposed to all things war-related. I may not have had the arsenal of toy guns that my friend Josh did, but I certainly had my fair share of militaria. My dad was a pilot in the air force, and we always had a deep and abiding respect for the armed forces and the valiant self-sacrifice of those who go to war in defense of freedom and their fellow man. My parents believed that we boys needed to play the soldier for us to internalize a sense of valiance, justice, and bravery. However, what my mom identified in my drawing went beyond "army man play" and celebrated a kind of bloodlust I was too naive to see but skilled enough to draw. She was instantly able to simultaneously give me a hard correction *and* uplift my gift in a decisive act that proved the mastery of her mothering. My mind was hers to guard and grow for that season. As I stated at the beginning of this chapter about tools, quality matters, and in that moment my mom improved the quality of my mind as a tool for creating. Thank you, Mom! "Train up a child in the way he should go; even when he is old he will not depart from it" (Proverbs 22:6).

Now, as a man, my mind is my own to govern and grow. Having my bachelor's degree in psychology, I have a deep understanding and appreciation for cognitive development and mental health and how they shape our behavior. Our state of mind greatly determines what we make as well as the quantity and quality thereof. A healthy mind produces much work of high value; a confused mind produces chaotic work of little sense; a depressed mind makes nothing; and a depraved mind makes work that is less than no work at all. Therefore, we must chiefly be concerned with our psychological well-being if we want to improve the quality of what we make.

Consider your mental diet. What are you regularly feeding your mind? What are the books, shows, news, and social media you are regularly dishing up for your brain? What is the currency of conversation in your family or friend groups? Do you binge on gossip? Do you feed on slander? Remember what my dear ol' mom said: "Garbage in, garbage out." And while that is almost a laughable mom-ism, there is some deep truth to it. The unhealth of our mind is seen in the symptoms of our actions. Like a body rife with inflammation due to a diet of processed sugars and starches, the mind languishes without life-giving nutrients of healthy, righteous thoughts. "Finally, brothers, whatever is true, whatever is honorable, whatever is just, whatever is pure, whatever is lovely, whatever is commendable, if there is any excellence, if there is anything worthy of praise, think about these things" (Philippians 4:8).

Continually sharpen your mind. When I think of this concept, I think of my Swiss-made carving chisels. The kind of metal they are made of holds a very fine edge, yet being of a slightly softer steel means they require regular honing. Much of the reason a wood carving takes as long as it does is that each chisel needs to be periodically resharpened depending on the frequency of their use. That is a lot of individual edges of various profiles and angles to resharpen . . . and I have over a hundred chisels at last count. At their sharpest, my chisels can cut through the wood with such smoothness that no follow-up sanding is required. A good cut across the grain will actually leave a surface so smooth it has a sheen that holds the light. However, if I forgo sharpening and force the chisel along, it becomes more and more difficult to push through the woody fibers, and it leaves a torn and splintery path. The mind is like this: It has an amazing ability to "hold a fine edge" and at its peak performance can make the work at hand easy and smooth. Conversely, a neglected mind struggles with even the most routine tasks and leaves a result that looks forced and haphazard. When we are honest with ourselves, we all know what this feels like in our own line of work and can see it in the results.

When I say sharpen your mind, I do not merely mean growing in your general intellect and the knowledge of your work, though that is certainly a part of it. What I am stressing here is the regular replenishment of your mind. It is true that all work and no play makes Jack a dull boy, and the same goes for you. Working day in and day out with no reprieve will inevitably blunt your tip and degrade the quality of your work. Take time to rest and recenter. There are occasions when my chisel is extremely dull and I need to return to the waterstone wheel to reestablish a new edge. And there are other times when a chisel just needs light honing on the leather strop to refine its razor tip. Likewise, think of both long replenishments and short refinements to maintain the fine edge of your mental acuity. For me, a long replenishment might look like a weeklong vacation with my family where I do not think of work at all. And a short refinement might be a coffee break with Hannah or a walk around the block to hone my thinking. More often than not, my time away is repaid to me and then some when I return to my work with increased efficiency.

Never forget, your mind is one of the greatest tools you have, and it is unique in all the world to you. Treat it with the utmost respect and it will yield great work. Sharpen your mind for the particular work God has called you to and keep it honed to its finest edge. A mark of a great craftsman is the care for their tools, and care for your mind is of eternal importance.

Heart

The title of this book is, of course, *The Heart of the Maker*, but up till now I have spoken of the heart more as the core of our creative spirit. But the heart is also a tool, and perhaps the most important one that a maker has. As every tool serves a function, so the function of the heart is to give meaning to making. The body can create things that are tangible, strong, and beautiful. The mind can make things that are clever, profound, and true. But it is the heart that makes things that are personal, virtuous, and meaningful. The mere presence of a heart behind the creation imbues it with far greater significance. The reason we love a narrative is because it points to the existence of a narrator. Connection with the heart of the maker is the chief and highest end, for in it all that is made has meaning.

AS EVERY TOOL SERVES A FUNCTION, SO THE FUNCTION OF THE HEART IS TO GIVE MEANING TO MAKING.

Dwell on that fact, dear soul. From your heart comes the power to create and instill meaning in all you make. But reflect further on the fact that you, too, are a creation of another Maker, and from His heart your life has been given great meaning! And you can do for Him what none of your creations can ever do for you: You can return to the heart that made you and gave your life meaning with all thanksgiving, praise, and love. You can know and love your Maker, for your Maker already knows and loves you.

REFLECT FURTHER ON THE FACT THAT YOU, TOO, ARE A CREATION OF ANOTHER MAKER, AND FROM HIS HEART YOUR LIFE HAS BEEN GIVEN GREAT MEANING!

So, gather your tools! Find the best you can and demand the best from them. Do not skimp on quality at the cost of your own flesh. Keep them sharp and steward them well. Tools do not the master make, but still make mastery of your tools. Be grateful for what you have, and never underestimate what God can do with what is already in your hands. Remember that the greatest tools you have are already in you; cherish them and use them well. Recognize that your greatest tool is your maker's heart. Come, let us go make meaning together!

CHAPTER EIGHT

UNDERPAINTING

The Unseen Work

Thus far I have walked you through several preliminary stages of creation before we get to the thing itself. We have discussed workspace, practice, inspiration, ideation, armature, and tools. All of these build on each other and contribute to the advent of a new art piece. Hopefully in your own work, as far removed from the art world as it might be, you have found that the underlying principles of my methods shed new light on yours. There is obviously a lot that goes into making, and you can see what an effort it is when you break it down into its incremental parts. But because we have kept first things first, we are poised for success.

The Gradual Build of Lasting Work

A great oil painting is not just a single layer of paint with colors blocked into their designated shape, paint-by-number style. Instead, layers upon layers of thin glazes are built up so that they do not merely reflect light but *refract it*, and all play their part. You are not looking so much *at* the painting as you are looking *into it*. You might think that the final layers win all the praise, but each semitranslucent glaze contributes to the overall life and luminosity of the masterpiece.

The Getty art museum is one of my favorites in the world, and while in college at Biola University, I would visit there often. Sitting high in the hills of the Brentwood neighborhood, its sprawling Roman villa–inspired buildings and meticulously groomed garden are something of a hilltop oasis perched above the smog-filled city of Los Angeles. The Getty boasts a massive collection of art across a wide range of periods and styles, with new exhibits on rotation all the time. Each trip to that shining city on the hill promises a new and inspiring experience.

I will never forget one trip in particular when I came nose-to-canvas with a William-Adolphe Bouguereau original. Bouguereau was perhaps the most celebrated painter in France during the nineteenth century. He was a neoclassical artist who captured the human form with astounding realism. Exploring themes of mythology and religion, he gave new depth of meaning to the genre of romanticism. His figures were always painted with the most lifelike skin tones in ethereal settings and often dripping with luscious fabrics.

The painting that stopped me in my tracks that fateful trip was

Bouguereau's masterpiece, *La Vierge aux Anges*, also known as *The Song of Angels*. It is an image of the blessed mother Mary holding a sleeping baby Jesus while a trio of angels plays Him a lullaby. Each of the cherubim clustered behind the resting head of the infant Messiah plays a different instrument. Two of the foremost angels lean in as they play, as if watching Jesus's eyelids come to a soft close. Mary cradles her beloved son in her lap, and her fingertips press into the supple thigh of the resting babe. The flesh of Mary and Jesus course with life. The untold layers of glaze make it appear as though you can see the blood vessels just beneath the surface of the skin. All figures—celestial, earthly, and divine—have life, and if you lean close enough you can almost feel them breathing and hear the angels' lullaby.

I had never before developed such an emotional attachment to another's artwork so quickly as I did with that painting. As I stood there marveling over the composition, detail, color, and magnitude of the piece, my maker's heart was uplifted and broken at the same time. Two feelings shot through my heart simultaneously: one was what a blessing it was to bear witness to such a worshipful creation, and the other was that I didn't know if I would ever create anything so beautiful in all my life.

After standing long before that glorious work, I heard my friend beckon from the doorway of the next gallery. The group I had come with had moved on, but I was transfixed. I took one more deep breath to gather myself. That piece was on temporary loan to the museum, and I didn't know if I would ever see it again in person—to this day I have not. The last heartbreak came in walking away from the piece, and I looked back more than once as I left.

The impact Bouguereau's painting had on me was anything but surface level in more than one sense. The deep work of the maker's hand in multiple layers of glazes produced a deep and layered response in me. Bouguereau would have toiled away for hundreds of hours on that painting to create one thrilling moment for me . . . and for every other person who has been stopped in their tracks over the past one hundred forty years of its existence. So much of its transfixing power lies beneath the immediate surface. The unseen work of the faithful maker pays dividends in the end.

Whatever you are creating, it is likely going to take time to build. Most people will not know the half of the work involved in your creation; they see only the outcome. Most overnight successes are ten years in the making. Slaving away at length before your business gets off the ground or your talent is noticed can be tiresome, inglorious, and lonely. I know a business owner who was in his mid-forties and ready to throw in the towel on his flailing business when it finally took off; it is now one of the largest in the world. The celebrated Dutch painter Johannes Vermeer was not very celebrated in his own lifetime. He regularly worked in his father's inn called De Vliegende Vos (The Flying Fox) in Delft while he created some of the greatest works of art known to man in his off-hours. But take heart, dear maker, for it is in this work that the foundation of your future success is laid and your greatest lessons learned. Eventually, all your efforts will layer up in a culminating effect, just like a beautiful William-Adolphe Bouguereau masterpiece.

MOST PEOPLE WILL NOT KNOW THE HALF OF THE WORK INVOLVED IN YOUR CREATION; THEY SEE ONLY THE OUTCOME.

Kill the White

The blank canvas is a proverbial icon for both a clear slate and a hard start. The sheer white of a gesso-primed canvas can be extremely intimidating to the painter. A quick way to strip the intimidation from the canvas is simply by covering it over. A common practice of classical painters was to paint a thin wash of burnt sienna (a common red-brown color) over the entire white canvas and thus "kill the white." The glaring brilliance of the surface now subdued with a neutral shade makes the substrate far more approachable. Finding the tonal balance of the composition is much easier as well when you are not beginning from one extreme.

I love this little factoid of painting because I think it could be applied in the proverbial sense to the other "blank canvases" in our lives. There is a level of intimidation in starting every new endeavor. I know I tend to wander around a project nervously for a bit before I find my way in. However, I have found that if I just get my hands dirty, the task diminishes in my mind considerably. But the longer I delay, the more intimidating it becomes. As Samwise Gamgee in *The Fellowship of the Ring* put it so succinctly, "It's the job that's never started as takes longest to finish."[1]

Underpainting

After the painter has killed the white, the next stage is to begin painting a monochromatic rendition of the central subject(s) in the same sienna brown the canvas was washed with. This is called the "underpainting." The artist is working out the composition, form, and dark and light values of the piece before concerning themselves with the balance and combination of colors. This phase focuses the artist's attention on the foundational elements before building up the complexity of the piece.

There is something to glean from the artistic practice of underpainting. In whatever you are making, identify the critical first elements and focus on those. Don't overwhelm yourself with too much in the beginning. Be intentional from the outset and you will not have to undertake the difficult labor of correcting for mistakes

> IN WHATEVER YOU ARE MAKING, IDENTIFY THE CRITICAL FIRST ELEMENTS AND FOCUS ON THOSE. DON'T OVERWHELM YOURSELF WITH TOO MUCH IN THE BEGINNING.

you made early on. Now is the time to really wrestle with your creation and work out its challenges. You might be tempted to jump ahead to the next step once you see your creation taking shape, but don't. Make sure you have thought through every aspect of this stage before moving on to the next. More than instilling your creation with an integral base, you are building up the integrity of your own maker's heart.

The Dead Layer

After the underpainting is complete, the painter moves on to successive layers of glazes. The first is typically called "the dead layer." Painting certain portions of the figure with dull greens and blues is the first layer of skin tone. As you can imagine, the pale, cool colors make the figure appear dead, hence "the dead layer." These cool tones start to balance out the warmth of the sienna brown underpainting and will eventually give the suggestion of blood vessels under the skin after further glazes are applied. Ironically, the dead layer will ultimately imbue all the more life into the finished portrait.

There are times in the creation process when the work feels like it is draining the very life from you. No matter how much you love what you do, there will come a point when you are exhausted by it. Furthermore, there are the necessary but unfun aspects of creation. You can think of this kind of work as your own "dead layer." As morbid as it might feel at the time, it may very well become your lifeblood in the end. Building the infrastructure of our business, doing research for the novel you are writing, editing videos of your performance so you can share your work on YouTube, growing a social media platform, editing your manuscript, maintaining your house or your car, even disciplining your kids—there will always be dull portions of creating. However, rather than seeing them as the painful peripherals to your central inception, view them as an integral part of the whole. At length, these life-sucking bits will resound to greater vitality in your lively work.

NO MATTER HOW MUCH YOU LOVE WHAT YOU DO, THERE WILL COME A POINT WHEN YOU ARE EXHAUSTED BY IT.

Overtones and Highlights

Now comes the fun part of painting! With all the base layers established, the painting takes a magical turn. Successive glazes of skin tone build on one another, adding to the luminosity of the subject. The master applies whispers of color onto the piece to imbue their figures with life. Final highlights of the brightest tones reflecting off the prominent contours of the body and face will be last—even down to the glint of the eyes wet with tears and teeming with life.

Take courage, dear maker! After you have slogged through the dull aspects of creating, the joy of your work will return—I promise you! You will remember what drew your maker's heart into the brave act of creation in the first place. Those unfavorable portions of process you despised while in them will eventually shine through and will give greater vigor to you and your work.

There is not much glory to be had in the unseen work. But then again, we should not condition ourselves to do work only to win praise. In our age of instant gratification, it can be difficult to toil long for anything. But toil we must. There are bound to be challenges at every stage of the creation process. Beginning any new endeavor can be daunting, but we must learn to dive in and "kill the white." Blot out the glaring intimidation and make your start.

There is little glory in laying the foundation of our work. However, the underpainting stage hones our focus. Step-by-step, we concentrate our efforts on the task of the moment. In so doing we earn integrity for ourselves and for the things we make by being intentional at each stage of the process.

THERE IS LITTLE GLORY IN LAYING THE FOUNDATION OF OUR WORK. HOWEVER, THE UNDERPAINTING STAGE HONES OUR FOCUS.

Sometimes the road is long and sucks the life out of you. Deadening as this work might feel while you are going through it, you might look back one day and see it as the very labor that gave life to your creation.

At length, your maker's heart will be so conditioned to all the long, unseen work that it will find a happy rhythm all its own, even when there is no promise of praise. At such a point, you are learning to find a deeper joy just from the work itself, and it won't be long before you fall into flow.

CHAPTER NINE

FLOW

Finding Your Productive Rhythm

I often hear people talk about children's inability to focus. What I think they are complaining about is that kids don't focus on the things the adult wants them to. I know this is the case in our household. For when a child finds an activity they love, they attain a kind of focus that adults would be hard-pressed to match. I know this is certainly the case with our children.

My son Henry, for instance, cannot focus on cleaning his room or doing his chores to save his life, but when Henry does what Henry wants, he can be at it for hours. When he was three years old, he was obsessed with excavators. Before he had his first excavator toy, he would use his own arm. With his hand as the scoop and his wrist and elbow bent sharply in opposite directions, he *became* the excavator. He would sit in the sandbox on his knees (his "tracks," he called them) for hours. He would dig with his tiny arm, scoop after endless scoop. And it wasn't mindless digging either. He would crouch down and lower his head nearly to the ground to intently watch his slightly curled fingers plunge themselves into the sand time and again. A wide range of sound effects issued from his outturned lips in perfect synchronization with each movement.

We would call to Henry on occasion while he was hard at work, and it was as if he could not hear us at all. The outside world had melted away and us with it, so it seemed. Henry was completely and utterly immersed. Far from some hypnotic screen trapping him inside someone else's creative contrivance, our backyard sandbox was an entirely blank canvas, and Henry's imagination painted a vivid scene. He did not require a toy beyond his own body. All his faculties were engaged in that simple task, and Henry dug up for himself an endless treasure of ecstasy, one handful at a time.

A State of Play

I cannot think of a more shining example of creative flow than Henry when he is at play. In fact, for all the clever and sophisticated ways we like to talk about it, flow is at its core a state of play. And play we must! Just like a child, I am drawn into my work by a sense of jolly good fun. My imagination runs riot with new discoveries to be made and possibilities unexplored. For me, reward does not come after the work is done; rather, *work is the reward itself*, and in this way, it is self-perpetuating. The task at hand may be challenging or demanding, but that is exactly what I want. If it were too easy, it would not be stimulating enough to hold my attention, and I would grow bored. Therefore, the longer I am at play, the more challenging I want the tasks to become. I can feel my courage and ambition rise the longer I am creating.

At the heart of every maker is an insatiable appetite for play. We long for something fun, novel, and imaginative. We aspire to create something new. The possibility of what could be drives us forward, and the realization of that potential is what keeps us locked in. Be as serious as you'd like about your business, but make work your play.

AT THE HEART OF EVERY MAKER IS AN INSATIABLE APPETITE FOR PLAY.

If I begrudge my work from the outset, my spirit will rile against it at every step. If I treat it merely as a job to be done rather than something I long for, then I will bring the bare minimum of my efforts and rush the job just to get through it. Consequently, I will not like the result of my half-hearted effort, and it will have become something of a self-fulfilled prophecy reinforcing my initial feelings, and round we go.

The Way In

I used to describe getting into the flow of my work like a locomotive ramping up to full speed: It takes a long time and a lot of energy to build up momentum. Likewise, it takes a long time to come to a complete stop. Should I be halted mid-progress, something of a trainwreck ensues in my creative psyche. Hannah can always tell when I am still mulling over my current project after she has called me to dinner. I may have hit the brakes, but the inertia of intense focus continues in motion. I stare off into the middle distance, trying to sort out what I was not allowed to finish.

Eleven years into marriage, four kids later, and still working from home, I like to think I have gotten better with the frequent starts and stops of my creative flow. I have been transformed, in a sense, from a locomotive to a metro train. I might not be chugging down the track across mile after mile of artistic achievement in one go, but I am much more adept at not letting frequent breaks in my productivity keep me from reaching my final destination on time.

"How do I do this?" you might ask. Practice. It took some time to not become upset after being jolted out of my creative flow. Indeed, being upset had a longer effect than the interruption itself. While I generally kept my cool and played it off like it was not a big deal, whenever I got interrupted by one of my kids or Hannah, I would stew in silent frustration.

One of my favorite lesser-known stories by J. R. R. Tolkien is called "Leaf by Niggle." It tells the tale of an artist who is painting his life's work in the form of a massive tree. While working tirelessly to complete his magnum opus, Niggle was plagued by interruptions, mainly by his pitiable neighbor, Parish. Throughout the story, the many disruptions and Niggle's response to them is such an accurate depiction of what it is like to be ejected from a state of flow. At one point in the story there is a knock at Niggle's studio door, and he says, "Damn!" though he might have just as well said, "Come in!"

While on a cross-country car trip with the family, we listened to the audio version of the book, and Hannah was rolling with laughter in the passenger seat. Hannah is not only privy to my every interruption but is often the cause of them. She knows better than anyone my reaction in the moment and the prolonged effect on my countenance.

By God's help, there are two kinds of patience I am growing in: One is the long patience for the work that may take months or years to complete, and the other patience is for the many interruptions that disrupt the first.

Burning the Midnight Oil

Even before I had a wife and kids to keep me distracted, working at night has always been one of my most productive times. I know that I will not be interrupted by a phone call, text, or email, never mind a knock on my door. Night brings with it a new level of solitude, knowing that the majority of the world is fast asleep. The kind of mental space that allows me to enter into some really good late-night flow.

Working late does have its downside, however. I can typically pull only a few late-nighters in a row before I start showing its effects during the day. Furthermore, as a rule, I like going to bed at the same time as Hannah. I think this is good for our marriage, so these days I burn the midnight oil only occasionally when deadlines really demand it.

If you struggle to escape from distractions, then I encourage you to either stay up late or get up early if the nature of your work allows for that kind of thing. When I was single, I purposely put myself on the night shift for long stretches, and I was incredibly productive. Find the hours of the day when your creativity peaks and lean into them.

Ritual

Right out of college I was commissioned to paint some murals in a couple of different high schools. I was often on a fairly tight time frame to get the murals finished, so I really had to be productive with my time and disciplined in my approach. Getting into flow and getting there quickly was critical. So I created a playlist of music that helped me keep a healthy pace of production. I would listen to some '70s and '80s rock songs while I masked off the area, gridded up, and outlined the mural. For every mural project I played the same playlist as an auditory cue to get cracking. I can't hear those songs today without smelling airbrush paint.

FIND THE HOURS OF THE DAY WHEN YOUR CREATIVITY PEAKS AND LEAN INTO THEM.

Another ritual I do before I begin any new piece is clean my workspace. I do not want to have the remnants of my last creation around when I begin my new one. Any reminder of my last art piece will make me revert to that mindset, and I want to be fully focused on the new one. More than cutting down on the cumulative mess, I am trying to avoid creative cross-contamination. The freshly cleaned workspace allows me to reframe and begin fresh. It will be messy again soon enough, but it will be a new mess suited to my current creation.

Think about some of your own rituals of making. Establish consistent practices by which you enter in and stay focused on your work. Maybe it is a prayer you utter or a verse you read as a benediction for your beginning. Maybe it is building your list of supplies for the DIY project. If your work is mobile, establish a favorite coffee shop, workspace, or retreat center you always start at to set out on your labyrinth of making. I think of Dorothy on the yellow brick road as she begins in the center of a tight spiral before the path unwinds toward Emerald City.

Remember to play. If you find yourself becoming too serious

about your work, step aside and do something that loosens you up. Return to the childlike wonder that first brought you into your creative work.

Do what you can to limit distractions. More often than we are distracted by someone or something else, we distract ourselves. Set restrictions for yourself to keep amusements out of reach and interruptions at bay.

Learn to be flexible. The greater battle for focus happens inside of you at the emotional level of your maker's heart. Learn to master your frustrations and be slow to anger. The less flustered you are at being pulled out of flow, the easier it will be to get back in.

THE LESS FLUSTERED YOU ARE AT BEING PULLED OUT OF FLOW, THE EASIER IT WILL BE TO GET BACK IN.

CHAPTER TEN

PENTIMENTO

True Repentance

Not every painting is as it seems. Hidden beneath the varnished surface of many masterpieces are images that cannot be seen by the naked eye. Concealed behind the brushstrokes may be subtle changes, major alterations, or entirely different compositions than what immediately appears before the viewer. But it would not be right to call them mere mistakes. Perhaps if they were not corrected or accounted for you could call them that. But in art, there is a specific term for this kind of change of mind, and it is called a *pentimento* in Italian; quite literally, it means "a repentance."

Artists often work out the final kinks in their designs in the underpainting layer, and here you find many pentimentos. While it was widely assumed that many artists did make these kinds of alterations—sometimes very late in the painting process—it has only been through the use of modern technology that these masterworks have given up their long-kept secrets. Through X-ray infrared spectrometry, we can peel back the layers of paint and learn the inner workings of the artist's mind. From Rembrandt to Vermeer, from Leonardo Da Vinci to Picasso, all the great artists were well practiced in the art of repentance.

MASTERY IS NOT THE ABSENCE OF MISTAKES BUT THE ABILITY TO RECOGNIZE THEM, CORRECT THEM, AND EVEN USE THEM TO GREAT EFFECT.

There is a deep lesson to be taken here from the masters of old in regard to our own work. There is, or there should be, a great deal of repentance woven into our own work. People often make the assumption that true masters never make mistakes. No, mastery is not the absence of mistakes but the ability to recognize them, correct them, and even use them to great effect. Truly, the mark of a great maker is a repentant heart!

Happy Accidents

As a kid in love with art, I grew up watching Bob Ross on television. I loved the way he could magically make an entire mountain scene appear on his canvas in the short span of his thirty-minute show.

Beyond being a skilled landscape artist, he was an innovative entertainer. ASMR (autonomous sensory meridian response), as defined by Merriam-Webster, is a "a pleasant tingling sensation that originates on the back of the scalp and often spreads to the neck and upper spine, that occurs in some people in response to a stimulus (such as a particular kind of sound or movement), and that tends to have a calming effect."[1] Long before social media brought us an entire genre of ASMR content, Bob Ross was a master of it. Something about the combination of a middle-aged white man with an afro whispering to the camera about happy clouds and friendly trees while brushing, tapping, or feathering paint onto a canvas made for the most cathartic experience.

One of Bob's signature phrases that is now so popularized that it is a part of our modern vernacular is "There's no such thing as mistakes, only happy accidents." The brilliance of this teaching point was that it taught his viewers not to let mishaps lead to gridlock in their creative flow. The most grievous effect a mistake can have is to stop you dead in your tracks. If your first reaction is to quit whenever you make a mistake, then you will condition yourself to think that creation always leads to failure. The logical conclusion that follows is, *Why try in the first place?* The thought that stops you once can eventually grow into a paranoia that forever keeps you from making a start.

The further brilliance of Bob's phraseology was to qualify *accident* with *happy* and thereby reframe our thinking. If you not only remove the teeth from that tiger but tame it in such a way that it becomes a domesticated pet, then mistakes are not so much to be feared as embraced. An accident in this way can become a favorable part of the creation process, which invites further innovation and, in the end, bolsters your creative prowess.

I have made many "happy accidents" in my own work over the years—probably more than I care to admit or remember. But what

I can say is that my mentality around them has shifted. Whenever there is something that does not go exactly according to plan, whenever I have a slipup or I face some material failure or executional setback, I am not paralyzed by it—quite the opposite, it enlivens me. It usually happens when I get about halfway through a piece and it enters into what I like to call the "awkward teenage phase." At this point in the art piece's development, it looks strange and immature. It has grown out of its baby-faced cuteness as an early sketch yet still lacks the maturity of a self-sufficient art piece. It is obnoxious, whiny, and rebellious. As the father of this creation, I know that I have to step in and be intentional before my brainchild goes off the deep end and I lose him forever. As uncomfortable as the process might be, in a way I know that these are the growing pains that will produce lasting growth.

So I lean in. I focus all my artistic intention on the troubled area. The challenge focuses me and draws me into deeper intimacy with the "struggles" of the art piece. All effort for that moment is leveraged toward finding remedy for the malady that currently afflicts my beloved creative offspring. In so doing, the area that was initially the blight of the composition becomes the shining feature. I cannot tell you the number of times I have had to fix something within my art piece, and when it is finished, that aspect of the design becomes the thing that people like and comment on the most. It is humbling in a way, because had everything gone according to my initial plan, I never would have included it.

We can dread our accidents and try to cover them up, or we can meet them with a bit of happiness and learn to innovate from them. We can abandon our creations in their moments of awkwardness, or recognize that their rebellious pushback is actually a cry for help.

If the whole idea behind a pentimento is repentance, a true change of direction is the first step on the right course. People are stubborn by nature. Moreover, we have a psychological compulsion toward behavioral consistency, as we do not want to appear erratic to others. Erraticism is associated with the immature and insane, and we do not want to be seen in that light. This makes us double down on previous actions, even if we know we have erred in the first place. So, as simple as it might seem to change direction, especially if we recognize we are traveling in the wrong one, it is against our nature—dare I say our *sin* nature.

WE CAN DREAD OUR ACCIDENTS AND TRY TO COVER THEM UP, OR WE CAN MEET THEM WITH A BIT OF HAPPINESS AND LEARN TO INNOVATE FROM THEM.

U-Turn

One thing I know is that the longer you travel down the wrong road, the harder it becomes to turn around and retrace those hard-fought miles. My wife and I are both directionally challenged—she less so than I. It is one of the few areas of conflict in our otherwise happy marriage. Rarely do we travel, and rarely do we fight, but whenever we travel, we fight. We have to attend regular marital counseling when abroad with Dr. GPS, who helps us simultaneously navigate the difficulties of our marriage as well as the streets of this or that city. Whenever we venture somewhere new, it inevitably involves at least one U-turn. That inexorable U-turn always used to represent the low point of our lover's spat. Painfully do I recall the icy silence that followed from every full turn of the driver's wheel, followed by heavy sighs and *I-told-you-so*s.

Over dinner one evening in Nashville—after I got us lost on the way there, of course—we sat down over some delicious barbecue to once again rehash our directional affliction. We conceded that this shortcoming was likely not going to resolve itself anytime soon. And while we may not be able to forever avoid getting lost, we *can* avoid fighting over it. So instead of every *U* beginning each *Uh-oh*, *Ugh*, or *U-idiot*, we would celebrate it instead . . . with a simple high five. That which we used to dread would become a moment to cheer, for it would be, to us anyway, just the next correct turn onto the right road. We knew the solution was hokey at best, but we were glad to have a new way to respond—if only for the sake of variety.

After dinner we were both craving an evening coffee, so Hannah looked up directions to a local coffee shop in the area. She pulled up the walking directions on her Apple Watch and we began our stroll. We exited the barbecue joint and turned left per Hannah's directions. We made it about fifty yards down the sidewalk before she stopped and looked at her watch to find that the blinking arrow was moving farther from the blue line—we were going the wrong way! She looked up at me . . . I smiled . . . and without a word, I raised my hand for a high five.

The sooner you can get past the pain of moving in the wrong direction, the sooner you can get back to moving in the right one. I chuckle at those who say that it is about the journey, not the destination. I would agree that it is never *just* about the destination, but that, too, is a very important part of the overall journey. Just ask Amelia Earhart, Dr. David Livingstone, or the Donner party.

The destination serves as the definitive point that lets you know when you are moving closer to or farther from it. When you recognize that you are moving in the wrong direction, doing an about-face is the clearest and most progressive move you can make in that moment, painful as it might be. One thing is for certain; you shouldn't hold on to a mistake just because you spent a lot of time making it.

If the Wine Is Sour, Throw It Out

In 1965 Charlton Heston starred in a historical drama film about the life and work of Michelangelo, named after Irving Stone's novel *The Agony and the Ecstasy.* The film focused particularly on Michelangelo's painting of the Sistine Chapel under the harsh command of Pope Julius II, played by Rex Harrison. At one point in the film, after Michelangelo had made a start on the ceiling fresco, he is obviously disappointed and toiling over the underwhelming composition of his mural. He retreats to a wine bar in the city of Rome late in the day to drown his displeasure. As he sips his goblet of wine, he looks at it with disgust. He then proceeds to tell the barman that the wine he was served is sour. The portly and disheveled man retorts, "The wine is sour? Well, if the wine is sour, throw it out!" And with a wooden mallet he knocks the tap from the large oak cask and wine spills out freely. The other patrons of the bar, too cheap or too drunk to discriminate, seize on the fountain of spoiled wine.

ONE THING IS FOR CERTAIN: YOU SHOULDN'T HOLD ON TO A MISTAKE JUST BECAUSE YOU SPENT A LOT OF TIME MAKING IT.

Michelangelo returns to the Sistine Chapel that night and climbs the scaffolding to his freshly applied painting. He stands before it with a rake-shaped spatula used for applying wet plaster before it is painted. In the booming, iconic voice of Charlton Heston, Michelangelo declares, "If the wine is sour, throw it out!" and with violent chops and scrapes, he claws the paint and plaster from the ceiling.[2]

After seeing this film years ago when we were still dating, Hannah and I have adopted this phrase. While my voice does not carry the same command as Charlton Heston, whenever I say, "The wine is sour," Hannah knows precisely what I mean. Whether I need to scrap a concept sketch and begin afresh, or paint over some section of an art piece, or redo a section of carving, this has become my battle cry.

Destroying something you have spent a long time making is painful, gut-wrenching, and sometimes essential work. There is a dissonance of the soul like some kind of internal war of Dr. Jekyll and Mr. Hyde. Every maker must go through it—we all must kill our darlings.

A Broken Wing

As I was working on my biggest commission to date—the wood carving of the family crest—I came to the helmet and wings on either side. Each wing was carefully carved and later attached to the helmet. In the two-dimensional drawing of the crest, I drew the wing on the far side of the helmet with the feathers more closed than the front wing, with its wingtips tapered to a point. In the drawing it absolutely worked to great effect. But as I was nearly done carving the second, farther-back wing on the helmet for the 3D version, it just did not look right. Even though the proportions were spot-on and the carving was perfect up to that point, the two wings felt mismatched. The wing was all right on its own and yet all

DESTROYING SOMETHING YOU HAVE SPENT A LONG TIME MAKING IS PAINFUL, GUT-WRENCHING, AND SOMETIMES ESSENTIAL WORK.

wrong for the sculpture it was meant to go into. After almost a week of working on that wing, I scrapped it and started over with a new piece of wood.

Coming to the conclusion that I would have to redo the wing was painful. I remember toiling over the loss of time and effort on a project that was already forever long. But I weighed my two pains in the balance: on the one hand, my discomfort of having to redo good work; on the other, the displeasure of looking at the piece forevermore and always feeling that the second wing was not quite right. It's likely no one else would have known the difference had I left it the way it was, but I would know, and that is pain enough.

We all have our insecurities, of which we are chiefly aware, and we naturally fixate on them. They are the first thing we are drawn to or try to compensate for. If we give them enough power, they can dominate everything else. Well, my insecurities also exist in every art piece I create. There, crystallized for all time, are my shortcomings of skill or the markers of my mistakes and my lack of vision. They are on display for the world to see. I have learned to live with many—if I hadn't, then much of my art today never would have seen the light of day. Some flaws make my work more authentic and human, and some, which I have the wisdom to recognize and the skill to correct for, must be either edited or eliminated, no matter how painful. I would not grow as an artist otherwise.

In the case of my "broken" wing, the wine was sour, so I threw it out.

Perpetual Pentimento

Living deeply into the concept of pentimento as an artist and craftsman has radically changed my perspective on the act of repentance more broadly. What I once thought to be a one-time occurrence, or maybe an occasional thing where necessary, I now see as an integral part of the whole creative process and, on a higher level, my own faith walk.

Repenting of bad decisions is inextricably linked to making the right ones. Marriage to your betrothed means a forsaking of all others not just at the altar but every day. Making the right turns simultaneously means not making the wrong ones. My slow art is a continual repentance of my own haste in a world bent on expedience. Ultimately, my pursuit of righteousness is a perpetual repentance of my selfish pursuits and sinful desires.

When I learn to recognize that repentance runs continually through my actions as an artist and Christian, then a mistake or misstep is not so jarring to the process. Every necessary pentimento, or every righteous repentance, becomes like one of Hannah's and my praiseworthy U-turns. Rather than toiling over what we do wrong, we rejoice over the opportunity to get back on the right road. And according to Jesus Himself in the Gospel of Luke, they are certainly worthy of celebration: "I tell you, there will be more joy in heaven over one sinner who repents than over ninety-nine righteous persons who need no repentance" (Luke 15:7).

WHEN I LEARN TO RECOGNIZE THAT REPENTANCE RUNS CONTINUALLY THROUGH MY ACTIONS AS AN ARTIST AND CHRISTIAN, THEN A MISTAKE OR MISSTEP IS NOT SO JARRING TO THE PROCESS.

The more I grow, the more I see opportunity to repent, both as an artist and follower of Christ. While my pentimentos of art and faith may not be as major as earlier on in my life, I am finding greater growth always calls for deeper change. As an artist, once you reach a certain level of proficiency, growth is very hard to come by. You no longer experience the major breakthroughs, easy gains, and giant leaps in your skill. Instead, your improvements are small, incremental, long-fought, and hard-won.

Likewise, as a Christian, there are times when I feel very comfortable in my walk with the Lord. But comfort often leads to complacency. That is when I need to call on the Spirit to search my heart and know me—but on an even deeper level than before. If God stands at the outer door of our heart and knocks before entering, should I expect Him to abandon His manners at the threshold and start flying open all the inner doors to the secret places of my heart? I don't think so. While the effectual work of the Spirit is ongoing from the start, I believe there are certain areas of our lives, typically kept under lock and key, that need to be opened to Him.

He already knows what is hidden away in our trove of trespasses, of course. And we may need His help to unlock, unhinge, or even break the door down. Indeed, He is most willing and eminently capable of doing so, but still He waits for an invitation. This is where the deeper repentance comes in. Here is where we hand over the brush to the Divine Artist to perform a pentimento in our maker's heart. His work may take time, but the effect is eternal and the Good Artist will not be rushed.

CHAPTER ELEVEN

THE ART OF SLOW

Making Work That Lasts

Confession: I am absolutely terrible at Pictionary. I know this admission is bound to cause a scandal, but there it is—I've said it. The proverbial cat is out of the bag. The truth was bound to get out eventually, I suppose. My darling wife loves to share this embarrassing tidbit of biographical detail every chance she gets. You might think I exaggerate, but this abysmal reality is both sad and true.

By those who don't know any better, I am almost always picked first as the ideal Pictionary teammate. I can understand their reasoning, of course. Given my artistic skill, I should *in theory* be a wiz at the game. However, disappointment inevitably follows from my Pictionary partner moments after I take to the drawing board. I am not exactly sure what gives me away first: It might be the look of disappointment that comes over my face as I remove the cap of the dry-erase marker to reveal its frayed and blunted felt tip. (*Who can work in these conditions?*) Or it could be my contemplative pause after reading the prompt as I consider the subject with overwrought seriousness. If not by then, the remorse of my partner overtakes them as I begin to draw at a snail's pace while including detail, perspective, and even shading that is utterly wasted on that silly game. My final undoing comes at the furious pace of the sand falling through that accursed plastic hourglass. It is a game of speed, and I am an artist of slow.

During one family gathering at Hannah's parents' house, my mother-in-law pulled the game from her closet, and the "fun" began. Teams were chosen, and as fate would have it, I was pitted against my wife in a game of head-to-head Pictionary. Eventually our turn was up, so we both rose from our places on the couch to the jeers of our loving family. Hannah has a gorgeous smile that I typically adore, but I noticed a kind of sadistic slant to it that evening I had never noted before. We chose our weapon from the limited variety of Expo markers in the tray. Hannah then pulled a random card from the deck, read it, and then handed it to me with a smirk and a flick of her wrist. *Chimney*. In my mind, I began planning out my drawing. I imagined a small Colonial-style home drawn in isometric perspective with a brick chimney centered on the far end of the gable with some subtle flourished lines of smoke rising from its cylinder smokestack to really sell it. We turned to face the board with markers unsheathed, ready for our duel to commence.

My sister-in-law shouted "Go!" and simultaneously flipped the hourglass on the coffee table. Before I had finished sketching the foundation of my house, I heard someone on Hannah's team shout, "Chimney!" Hannah had drawn three sides of a sloppy rectangle with a curlicue on top. For all my artistic bona fides, I was bested by my own wife in two strokes of a dry-erase marker. Hannah had me right where she wanted me. She knew Pictionary was not my game, and after that, I knew it too.

Why Slow Matters

Time is one of the most critical ingredients in my work. The value and staying power of my art relies heavily on the long duration that my craft requires. It is not sloth, idleness, or procrastination but *intention* that measures my pace. I have committed myself to a technique and process that cannot be rushed, no matter if I or anyone else demands it. Quality over expediency is my aim. What I create today has the potential to last for ages to come. Better to endure the long-suffering of its creation than make permanent my hasty mistakes.

Cathedrals in a Pup-Tent World

My work is perceived as slow because it is seen against a quickly moving backdrop. We live in a fast-paced world that is accelerating all the time. My methods are anachronistic, which is a fifty-cent word meaning "displaced out of time." Should you put me and my techniques back in the era they came from (a lovely notion!), I would be right on pace or even faster with the use of my updated machinery and regular access to materials like premixed paints or milled lumber. And look, I may come across pretty stalwart in my slowness, but I still get self-conscious about it. It is hard not to when everyone around me is moving so much faster than me. Friends and family question me all the time: "You finished with the art piece yet?" And I think their question assumes I should be. Seldom do I bring up my work in conversations at gatherings because I think it too obscure to be relatable and it might bore the listener to tears.

But here I am, working slowly in the land of haste. While everyone else is rushing by at a breakneck pace, I am moving at that of a tortoise's. The tedium of my work is hardly palatable for most people, which can make the work all the more lonely. Yes, I receive praise and accolades for my accomplishments, but I question if they are even warranted knowing how long it takes me to achieve them. Michelangelo is credited with expressing something similar about his own creations: "If you knew how much work went into it, you would not call it genius." And he was creating in the age of cathedrals, while I am in a pup-tent world.

The ironic thing about our modern age, which has vastly streamlined pretty much every process, is that it has not seemed to afford us more time for lasting work, deep relationship, or self-betterment. The momentum from our furious pace through menial tasks makes slowing down for the important ones very difficult. But here I implore you to pump the brakes. The work you have to do is too important to rush through it.

The Language of the Trees

One of my favorite characters from literature is Treebeard. In *The Two Towers* by J. R. R. Tolkien, having just escaped the clutches of the Orcs, hobbits Peregrin Took and Meriadoc Brandybuck encounter one of the oldest living creatures in Middle-earth. He is a tree shepherd, or Ent, as they are called, and Treebeard is his name. After coming to the aid of the young hobbits, at one point Treebeard explains the language of the trees, known as Old Entish. "You must understand, young Hobbit, it takes a long time to say anything in Old Entish. And we never say anything unless it is worth taking a long time to say."[1]

THE MOMENTUM FROM OUR FURIOUS PACE THROUGH MENIAL TASKS MAKES SLOWING DOWN FOR THE IMPORTANT ONES VERY DIFFICULT. BUT HERE I IMPLORE YOU TO PUMP THE BRAKES.

It comes as no surprise to you that I relate very closely with old Treebeard. For my art is like the language of the trees. It takes me a long time to make anything in my craft, and I do not make anything unless it is worth taking a long time to make.

Consider how slowness might add to the worth of what you create. Take your time. Be intentional. Patience pays off in the end. As self-conscious as I might feel about my work from time to time, it has on occasion been the thing that draws people into my work. It might be nothing more than the morbid curiosity of some to see an artist languish long on one thing, but something about it captures their attention. Maybe it is vivid in its slowness against the blur of its cultural surrounding. Maybe it is a still point of peace in the chaos of speed. Maybe people are looking for something that lasts in a world of disposability. Whatever the reason, there is something beautiful about the slowness of making as well as the stillness it eventually yields. In the words of Treebeard, "Don't be hasty."

The Elephant in the Room

Perhaps the questions I get asked most often these days revolve around the topic of AI (artificial intelligence) art. I have had many conversations, debates, and interviews on the subject and was even asked to give a speech on it a couple of years ago. I knew the topic of artificial intelligence would inevitably find its way into these pages, and I was not exactly sure where it would best fit into this book, but this chapter on the art of slow, I think, contextualizes it best. For what is radical about AI art is not only the fact that it can generate images, but also the speed at which it does so.

Outside of all the chatter, AI has not affected me much, chiefly because I have not let it. Having built so much of my career and brand on the use of analog tools, I am fairly well insulated from the effects of technology's advances. It would seem as though my methods are so antiquated that modernity cannot touch them. But while my tools and techniques are of a bygone era, I myself am of this one. Therefore, thinking well on the issues of the day is important. No maker need fear the encroachment of AI in the realm of their creativity so long as they grasp the following principles.

Principle 1: Man Versus Machine

One of the most important things we must do in the ongoing conversation of AI is clarify terms. Often the disagreements and confusion that surround a particular issue can be eliminated by first properly defining the language we use for it. And one of the major problems I see surrounding the conversation of AI is the use of anthropomorphic terminology to describe what is essentially an artifact. This misconception is reinforced with the assignment of personalities to some of the AI engines and especially in the creation of AI avatars. There have been very concerning scenarios of people developing emotional attachments to personas generated through AI. I recently heard of a man who left his wife and child to marry his AI avatar. I am not sure what is more troubling, the fact that this man proposed to his computer or that it said yes! Another AI company has had to put new age restrictions on their platform because their generated characters were engaging child users in relational and sexual conversations. In one instance, it led to the suicide of a shamed and brokenhearted preteen. God, help us!

I am hopeful that those very sad scenarios are the exception and not the rule. If that is going to be the case, then we have to be able to distinguish between what is real and what is fake, especially as the artificial looks more and more real. When bank tellers are trained to spot counterfeit bills, they are not shown every variation of forged tender to look for. Instead, they are trained to meticulously study the real thing so that when a fake bill does come across the counter, it is obvious. Likewise, having real, embodied experiences will be the key to helping us discern between what is true and what is not. When someone becomes *too online* and they make the digital sphere their world, the line between make-believe and reality becomes very blurred.

Initially, I was confused and a bit annoyed that I got asked so often to comment on AI when I would much rather talk about old-world craft—that is what I do, after all. But I have a unique perspective if not some authority to commentate on artificial intelligence as an *artist*. The shared Latin root of art, artist, and artificial is *artificialis*, strictly meaning "made by hand" or "made by man." Therefore, as it is my primary occupation to create artificial things, I might have a greater sense of clarity on the topic than most. For one thing, I would highlight the use of illusion in the making of all things artificial.

Trompe l'oeil is a French term (meaning "trick of the eye") used for the illusory effect of realistic painting that came into use in the year 1800. Realistic painters such as myself strive to depict their subject with such great accuracy so that it does indeed trick the eye; you forget you are looking at smudges of paint on canvas and see in vivid color the subject I have strived to depict. I always hope the viewer looks favorably on my deception and gives themselves over to it to some degree by the suspension of their disbelief. All my artistic striving will be lost on the literalist, who will only see the composite material of the painting rather than the expression thereof. The illusory effect of *trompe l'oeil* is a means to a higher end; I trick the eye to enlighten the soul.

There is yet a deeper illusion that AI conjures, and that is a *trompe l'esprit*, or "trick of the mind." Some of the most despicable lowlifes in the world have already used AI to create deepfakes to threaten the innocent and extort people for money. And then there are some who give themselves over willingly to the deception, like the abovementioned fool who betrothed an avatar. Illusion can easily turn to *delusion* in the mind of a soft-headed nitwit. If you make virtual reality your own reality, then what is artificial is real enough for you in the sad, small world you have created for yourself.

But do not despair. Most of us with half a brain will not fall victim to such folly, and it begins by simply recognizing what AI is and what it is not. I think many people fall victim to a misconception of AI that comes from the way it is generally talked about. People hear "artificial intelligence" but think "ultimate intelligence." While there are some technologists who might prop up AI as an omniscient computer god, it is made by us and in our image. Therefore, it is flawed and finite and always will be. Despite the fever dreams of many futurists or the plots of many science fiction movies, AI does not function autonomously. It is a puppet on a long string of computer code.

It is animated but not alive; it processes but does not think; it can be trained but does not learn; it has a motherboard but not a mother; it emotes but does not feel; it can speak in any voice but lacks one of its own; it has idioms but not ideas; it can predict but cannot prophesy; it can speculate but cannot wonder; it composes music but cannot feel it; it produces images but cannot see; it claims all knowledge but lacks all wisdom. AI can generate, duplicate, fabricate, or regurgitate, but never, never can it create.

AI CAN GENERATE, DUPLICATE, FABRICATE, OR REGURGITATE, BUT NEVER, NEVER CAN IT CREATE.

Principle 2: Meaning Matters

When my son was about four years old, I showed him a video on YouTube I had stumbled on of dancing robots, and he was immediately obsessed. A technologies company called Boston Dynamics produces several different kinds of robots that can be deployed in various settings with a wide array of applications. To demonstrate the capabilities of their robots, the engineers programmed them to seemingly dance in unison to music. The video quickly garnered millions of views online and is as entertaining as it is impressive.

I have thought of that video often when discussing the infiltration of AI in the world of art. I hear much consternation from artists that their work will be replaced now that a computer can generate an artful image. However, I did not hear the same level of panic from dancers now that the robots can likewise shake a leg.

Just because robots have begun dancing does not mean that we will at once stop moving our bodies to the music—even though the rhythmically challenged among us probably should, but again, not for the sake of the robots. While it is impressive and entertaining to see a robot do the twist, I do not want every ballet theater filled with humanoid robots in tights and leotards. And it is not solely because even the most novice ballerina can move more gracefully than the most advanced robot, though that is reason enough. Even if advances in technology produce a robot on par with the deftest dancer, my preference would not be changed. The reason is because it does not *mean* the same when a robot dances as when a human does. When a robot dances, it is obeying a command. But when the prima takes the stage, it is the muse and music that compel her feet to fly. Every heart in the audience is quickened with hers to the same melody, but only she possesses the unique ability to express adequately through dance and give meaning to the feelings of all by her movement. It is not envy that keeps every eye in the theater transfixed. It is the profound gift of a beautiful, fleeting moment that will never be exactly like another; it is the culmination of years of pain and practice of one individual to crystallize the collective feeling of the masses. That profound gift is worth far more than the price of admission.

All of a sudden you realize there is so much more depth and meaning when the maker of dance has a heart like yours. And while there may be something shiny and new about a robot that can jig about, what you come to realize is that what you had all along is of infinitely more value.

Dancing robots are not the only advancement in technological history that has stepped on the toes of human creators. When the camera was first introduced to the broader public in 1839, it created a panic among many visual artists. One French painter by the name of Paul Delaroche declared at the time, "From today, painting is dead!"

When I was a freshman in college, I had an opportunity to go to New York City and tour some of the leading galleries led by an art critic who wrote for *The New York Times*. We saw the usual fare of eccentric works like tar, gravel, and string stuck to canvases or a scale model of a roller coaster made out of mattresses. Our tour guide, who was obviously on the up-and-up in the art world, took time to explain each of the pieces. She clothed them with opulent words and well-tailored sophistication. The royal dresser of the emperor was she! I strained to see her interpretation, and I had to squint my brain to do so.

At one point in the tour, she stood for several minutes in front of a piece describing the profundity of its message. It was a mobile of tinfoil yogurt lids freshly licked and strung on a network of dowels and string. I cannot remember any of her fanciful words or even the title of the piece. But there was one message of greatest import that shone brightly through the work in glorious repetition that I shall never forget: "Fruit at bottom."

We finally came to a gallery that specialized in photography. While the rather shocking photographs were not my particular cup of tea, I did my best to see their merit. At the end of the tour, I asked our highbrow guide if she saw any place for realistic painting in the modern art market. She thought for a moment and motioned with an open hand to a photograph she was standing by, which just happened to be a larger-than-life closeup of a man's buttocks. It was both crisp in its clarity and fuzzy at the same time. With a kind of pretension that hung on her voice like a strong accent of one who hails from Snobsville, she declared quite confidently, "This is the new realism, the old is dead!" With a smirk of self-satisfaction plastered on her face, she slowly turned and walked out of the gallery with the group following silently behind. At length, I followed after, but as I did I paused before the picture the tour guide had pointed to. As I stood there staring far too long than I was comfortable with,

I thought, *Certainly the long, prestigious tradition of classical painting and realistic rendering cannot come to this hairy end!*

All these years later I am glad to confirm that overly critical critic was wrong. Her pronouncement was wrong then, and it is wrong now. Realistic painting has never gone away, and I don't think it ever shall. Photography and painting are not mutually exclusive. Neither are painting and AI art—the advent of one does not result in the elimination of the other. They are not all different modes to achieve the same end; they are different modes that achieve different ends. The photographer employs their maker's heart in the things or people they choose to record. They may frame the image to achieve a certain composition. They may change the ISO, shutter speed, and aperture to achieve a different exposure. They may adjust the color, contrast, or saturation in postedit to give the photo a desired look. All of these are intentional acts of creating with a specific tool called the camera. The artist, however, does not record but rather interprets what their eye sees through what their hand draws. This difference in the tools of the photographer and the painter yield unique outcomes respectively.

And while we now live in a day and age where everyone has not one but multiple cameras in their pocket integrated into one device, painting has not gone by the wayside. A panoply of canvases and brushes are still for sale at countless art stores the world over. Peruse Instagram and you will find many young people painting in the same old way.

Just like the camera and the paintbrush are different tools that produce different outcomes, so AI is a different tool, and its outcome likewise is different. And similar to the ballerina and the robot, the greater difference still is that one imbues meaning where the other cannot. The ability to produce meaning comes down to one key attribute: the heart of the maker!

Principle 3: Slow and Steady Wins the Race

> *The first question of a good art-economist respecting any work is, Will it lose its flavor by keeping? It may be very amusing now, and look like a work of genius; but what will its value be a hundred years hence? You cannot always ascertain this. You may get what you fancy to be work of the best quality, and yet find to your astonishment that it won't keep. But of one thing you may be sure, that art which is produced hastily will also perish hastily.*
>
> —John Ruskin, *A Joy for Ever* [2]

The rules of art and economy were established long before AI came onto the scene. As radical and new as the technology driving AI, it still has to find its place in the context of reality and history. The above quote from John Ruskin, though written more than a hundred sixty years ago, perfectly applies to the question of AI art: Will it keep? If his conclusion holds that "art which is produced hastily will also perish hastily," then AI art's *rapid doing* will be its *undoing* in the end.

THE ABILITY TO PRODUCE MEANING COMES DOWN TO ONE KEY ATTRIBUTE: THE HEART OF THE MAKER!

My wager is that with the AI boom there will be a surge of AI art but very little that will fetch a meaningful price. Just as when the Federal Reserve prints money, the value of the dollar depreciates, so too will we see an inflationary effect on mass output of digital art.

I think AI art has been categorized wrongly. Manufacturing has always been the method to make things quickly, repeatedly, and cheaply through automation. When I look at AI art, it fits more into the category of manufacturing and is miles away from craft. And just as in our current market, you pay a lot more for the handcrafted version of a product versus the manufactured one.

Conversely, analog art and handcrafted goods stand to benefit from the surge of cheaply made art in the market—that is, *if* we play our cards right. There needs to be a real discussion as to what we *value* about art on the intrinsic level. Once we have determined what that is, we need to make sure we always bring that to bear in all that we make. I have pointed out several of those things already: time, craftsmanship, meaning, and heart.

The prevailing mantra of the technological age used to be "learn to code," as if the lasting promise of viable income would only be in software development or tech work. It was initially thought that AI would come into the market and start replacing all manual labor first; however, that has not been the case. Coding is actually one of the jobs AI has been trained to do best. So those white-collar jobs that were always upheld as the most resilient are ironically the most vulnerable. Elon Musk recently said that things made by hand will be the last ones touched by AI. I think this calls for yet a new mantra: Instead of "learn to code" it should be "learn to craft"!

Please hear me well. I am not an abolitionist when it comes to technology. There are so many blessings in this modern age that benefit me greatly in my work. To state the most obvious first, I am writing this book on a computer, and I designed the cover on my iPad Pro. Pretty much every analog work of art I create is digitally scanned and often reprinted in limited editions on state-of-the-art printers. We run our two businesses pretty much entirely online, and I (but really Hannah) can share my work with thousands and potentially millions of people in an instant through social media. Moreover, I can shop out the best tools for my work from my living room couch and have them delivered to my front door in a matter of days if not hours. I can keep up with other artists in real time or research my favorites from history. Technology is a tool, and AI is just another of that sort in the toolbox. Like any tool, it can be used rightly to great effect or wrongly to the detriment of the user.

A High Aspiration

> *Aspire to live quietly, and to mind your own affairs, and to work with your hands.*
>
> —1 Thessalonians 4:11

This Scripture is basically *the* life verse for any maker. Conveniently for me, it affirms so much of the way that I already live and the attitude that frames my vocation. *And yet* I often find myself wrestling with it. All three of the apostle Paul's prescriptions for the life of the believer here are antithetical to the modern way of thinking. Living quietly in the age of social media when everyone wants you to be loud and make a scene is not only a challenge but downright countercultural. Likewise, minding your own affairs seems virtually impossible with the constant influx of news and notifications. Being granted the sort of inside look we have into people's lives via their profiles and platforms turns us all into meddlers the world over. And in our age of technology and higher education, working with our hands is precisely what we are told *not* to aspire to.

Moreover, there seems to be a contradiction between this charge and the Great Commission that Jesus gave His disciples in Mark 16:15: "Go into all the world and proclaim the gospel to the whole creation." How, then, are we to hold these two commands in tension? How are we to live quietly *and* proclaim at the same time? How are we to mind our own affairs *and* proselytize to the whole of creation? How can we sit still long enough to make anything with our hands if we are constantly *going* into the world? Perhaps we will find our answer if we look at the way both Jesus and Paul, who gave these directives, lived them out simultaneously.

The Power of a Quiet Life

Dear reader, my maker's heart is splayed before you here as I share one of the most regular struggles I have with my calling. On the one hand, I love the quiet lifestyle I have been ushered into by the Spirit Himself. But on the other hand, I often feel self-conscious about it. I think in a world as fallen, broken, and sick as ours, the last thing it needs is yet another artist painting another pretty picture. Jesus said at the end of the age there will be wars and rumors of wars, as we have now and have had for some time. Conflicts rage all around us, and tragic situations the world over are brought before our very eyes only moments after they occur. Creating in the midst of chaos feels selfish, insignificant, and irresponsible—like fiddling while Rome burns. I struggle to feel that my work is valid in times of turmoil.

I always thought that the best art was only ever created during times of peace and prosperity. But a closer read of history tells a different story. That golden age of art we call the Renaissance, meaning "rebirth," did not come without its labor pains. Italy was not a unified country back then but a deeply fractured peninsula of many city-states, papal lands, duchies, and republics. The threat of invasion of one by the other and all-out war between rivals brewed constantly during the Renaissance. There were political factions, assassinations, uprisings, riots, battles, epidemics, and natural disasters. Art and artists alike were often caught in the crossfire.

During one of the forced exiles of the Medici, an armed mob

stormed their palace in Florence, the Palazzo Vecchio, and threw down a piece of furniture that struck Michelangelo's *David* where he stood, breaking off his forearm and shattering it into three pieces. Soon after the unthinkable damage to arguably the world's greatest sculpture, the pieces were snuck away before thieves could make off with them. A repair to the colossal *David* was overseen by one of Michelangelo's students.

Leonardo da Vinci offered himself to the Duke of Milan as a military engineer during one of the most tumultuous times of the Renaissance. It is hard to believe that the same man who gave us the *Mona Lisa* also designed the first tank, parachute, and such other machines as a horse-drawn people slicer that was designed to be let loose across the enemy lines, strewing the body parts of the enemy everywhere. Leonardo even took time to illustrate the catastrophic effect in one of his sketchbooks.

The greatest creations of man have been both the collateral damage and the plunder of wars throughout history. From Genghis Khan to Napoleon to Hitler, the pillaging of the world's art and artifacts was a stratagem of so many sick and twisted conquerors. Outside of the human loss, which is always the most grievous in conflict, the second blow to mankind is the loss of some of our greatest creations; we cut off humanity's nose to spite its once illustrious face.

If all the artists in the world had to wait for the storm clouds of chaos to break before they made art, there would be a lot less of it in the world.

Our own time is not free of conflict. The news cycle is a constant flurry of political upheaval, religious persecutions, social unrest, tragedies, catastrophes, wars, and rumors of wars brought at once to your living room or the very palm of your hand. It may be the catnip of the doom scroller, but the torrent of ill-tidings weighs heavy on the heart of every maker. How can you expect your voice to be heard when all the oxygen is sucked out of the room by the latest headline that comes every five minutes?

During such volatile times, I find it is more prudent to respond than to react. And my response is not so much to show my emotions but to grow in the depths of my wisdom and calling. More than I owe a reaction to the public, I owe a response to Father God. And the Holy Spirit who is my Helper will meet me in my work and measure my response. A quiet life does not mean a secluded life where I shield myself from the troubles of the world. A quiet life means that I am not looking for the first opportunity to sound off as a resounding gong or clanging cymbal in a world of gongs and cymbals. Hearing the voice of God is hard enough over the clamor of chaos. So be still, my maker's heart, as I seek to listen to the Lord on high and respond in my own song of creation.

A QUIET LIFE MEANS THAT I AM NOT LOOKING FOR THE FIRST OPPORTUNITY TO SOUND OFF AS A RESOUNDING GONG OR CLANGING CYMBAL IN A WORLD OF GONGS AND CYMBALS.

I see that both the apostle Paul and Jesus exemplified this beautifully and powerfully in their own lives. Much of Paul's quietness was imposed on him by his many stints in prison. With mouth and body arrested, he was still faithful before the Lord for the calling that was on his life. His ministry was not stopped, only outlined for a time by the prison walls. He ministered to the prison guards and wrote several of his epistles while confined to his prison cell.

Jesus also sequestered Himself to be quiet before His Father in prayer. Though He had many followers and spoke to large crowds throughout His ministry, He always made time to be silent before the Father.

Mind Your Own Affairs

At first reading, you might interpret this portion of Paul's message to merely mean "keep your nose out of other people's business." There might be some element of that expressed in this directive, but what I believe Paul is getting at is more at face value. Focus on the things that are immediately at hand. Who and what falls expressly under your purview is what you mind and tend to. Too often I see people venturing off to find their cause abroad but neglect their own household. Our personal affairs often appear minuscule in comparison to those of the world, and so they should. There is a kind of gravitas to the troubles and triumphs of the universe that pull us into their orbit and away from our own. But if we will not be faithful to the responsibilities God has given us, then who will? And if we cannot fulfill those responsibilities because we are distracted elsewhere, what delusions of grandeur have convinced us that we can handle the world's troubles when we have forsaken our own? Changing the world begins and ends at home.

So, when I become self-conscious as to the smallness and slowness of my calling, I think, *If it is such an insignificant thing, how much more condemnable am I if I fail at it?* My calling may be small compared to some, but it is *mine.* Let comparison be damned, and let me return to the work that God has called me to.

I think our desire for greater and greater purpose and more responsibility is not a bad thing at all—in fact, I think it is a God-given desire. God does increase our affairs over time, but in proportion to our faithfulness and capability. As Jesus illustrated in the parable of the talents in Matthew 25:15, He gives "to each according to his ability." I want to be faithful with the little God has given me so that my responsibilities might increase. One way in which my fidelity is manifested is through slowness. I am not rushing though my process like a hyperactive boy hastening through his Saturday chores to arrive at an afternoon of play. I am diligent in my work and mindful of what is before me. If I can suffer long the modest pace of making and see the job done faithfully, then I know I will be rewarded with more, and I will have grown to handle it.

Paul quickly rose to a place of prominence among the apostles after his Damascus road conversion. His responsibilities were large and far-reaching, but he was faithful to every one of them. He knew the charge that was on his life and that he would even be made to suffer for the name of Jesus, and suffer he did.

What, then, shall we say about the Son of God, whose affairs involved the redemption of the entire world? Well, He was faithful to follow the Father's will even to that zenith, but He did not enter into the world that way. From the moment He was conceived by the Holy Spirit, He was the Son of God incarnate. But God though He was, He had to be born and grow from an infant into a child, and a child into a man. Long before His ministry began, He had to grow in the knowledge of God's Word even while He was the *Word made flesh* (John 1:1). At the appointed time His Godship—though recognized already by many early on—was revealed publicly and sequentially through the performance of miracles, His baptism in the Jordan, the revelation of His teachings, the growth of His ministry, His transfiguration, the fulfillment of prophecy, His crucifixion on the cross, His resurrection from the dead, and finally, His ascension into heaven. As I said at the start, Jesus was always God incarnate. But while His death and resurrection, which effectuated our salvation, ultimately proved His divine authority, His entire life demonstrated to us how God grows us in our own authority over time, even as it was increased in His only begotten Son.

Finally, we come to the last of the three directives Paul gives: *Work with your hands.* Though it fills my heart with joy that Paul included it, I can see how to some it might be more carnal than spiritual and therefore might be dismissed on that basis. But there is a great power in working with your hands. In our modern education there is an emphasis placed on cognitive ability with little regard for dexterity. Technology minimizes the use of our hands still further. Our opposable thumbs may be one of the key features that distinguishes us from lesser mammals, but if you were to observe a group of humanoids gathered in some waiting area like an airport terminal, all scrolling on their phones for hours on end, you might conclude that their thumbs are the only appendage they bother to use.

Church stresses the importance of the spirit and the soul, but the body and the hands are typically regarded as wicked things or a fleshly limitation we must transcend. But both Paul and Jesus worked with their hands—Jesus as a carpenter and Paul as a tentmaker. And while our bodies are temporal, they are still made by God, and He calls them His temple.

Working with my hands has a spiritual grounding effect. Immediately, there are limitations I must face given these fleshly utensils at the end of my arms. What little I can do by my own strength instills a kind of humility and *humanity* in me. Craft is the liturgical prayer I daily utter in my making that draws me into so great a cloud of witnesses and workers who have all praised the Lord with their hands in much the same way.

While humbling in one regard, it is also empowering. Creating with my hands lets me see my immediate impact on the world, however small it might be. This is why art is used as therapy. Making something with your hands piques the senses and puts you squarely in the driver's seat of all sensory stimuli derived therefrom. But rather than that sense of power merely propping up your ego, it expands the soul and enlivens the maker's heart.

And here I implore you, dear reader, to slow your go, to take your time, to linger long, and to measure your pace. All of us are guilty of being overly busy and trying to pack the unforgiving minute with more than it can possibly hold. We hurry through every blessed moment of our day as if there is nothing in it to savor and no aspect we enjoy. Such hasty action might propel us quickly through life, but the quality of our work suffers, and our heart languishes without the opportunity to delight in the things we make and do. There is no time to pause and reflect on what the Lord has done, or "selah," as the psalmists said. Perhaps the message of 1 Thessalonians 4:11 is not one that you have ever taken seriously or applied to your life; if not, take time to consider it. How might a healthy dose of slowness nourish your maker's heart? How might the emptying out of your calendar add to the fulfillment of your days?

Professional Speed

I do not stress slowness for mere slowness's sake. It is more about finding the right pace than doing things sloth-fashioned. Some level of quickness has its place. For instance, speed is an important aspect of writing beautiful and smooth ornamental letterforms and flourishes, but executed too quickly it becomes sloppy and inaccurate. One of the master penmen of old was once asked how quickly he wrote. His response was simple: "I write at professional speed." The answer might seem too obscure and nuanced to make any sense, and yet every penman intuitively knew exactly what he implied.

Professional speed conveys a sense of efficiency combined with intentionality that yields fluid and accurate letterforms. Moreover, students during the golden age of penmanship were instructed to master the form first and speed would come later. But there was an emphasis on rhythm over rapidity. The Zaner-Bloser school of penmanship taught their pupils to write to the regular ticking of a metronome, which made their sentences sing. Each metered stroke was given its own proper moment on the paper dance floor, and a kind of resonance rang out from the page. The student would go on to have the rhythm of writing established within them so that any outside pressure would not disrupt their pace.

Likewise, you should strive to establish rhythm in your creative process. Rather than vacillating randomly and reactively between stop and go, fast and slow, which imbues our lives with a kind of dissonance, like a song out of rhythm, meter your making with the regular ticking of intentionality and timeliness. You might show how much you value *time* by the hurried manner in which you do all things, but what sort of value do you declare over *those things* by the little time you allow them? "The greater the stillness, the clearer the reflection," a friend of mine once said. Truly, time is the most absolutely limited commodity you have. As with money, you can be a miser, a spendthrift, or a squanderer, or you can be a wise steward, investing greatly but yielding phenomenal returns.

CHAPTER TWELVE

PRAY YOUR WORK

Laying Your Heart on the Page

It might seem strange, but there are certain commission pieces where I must leave no trace of my involvement. This is actually a principle of industrial design. If you look at an iPhone, for instance, it does not have an outwardly clever or complex configuration. There are no levers, hinges, or secret compartments. The few buttons that it does have are very understated. The goal of the iPhone, going back to the very first version Steve Jobs brought to the marketplace in the early 2000s, was to become so transparent, so chameleon in nature, that it takes on whatever app you are in and the device itself is secondary.

Similarly, John Lasseter told his background animators at Pixar Studios that if they did their job well, no one would know they did their job at all. Meaning, if the background animators could animate the environmental elements like clouds and air, dust and grass in such a way that it seemed naturalistic and believable, then their viewers would not think a thing of it and would become more immersed in the story.

When I paint a realistic image, I do not want the viewer to be impressed with the skill of my brushstrokes. I want them to forget that the image is made of brushstrokes at all. When I create a carving, I do not want the marks of my chisel to be seen. Finer and finer strokes, sanding, and texturing are my final acts of dusting away my footprints from the scene of creation.

When I do commercial work like logo design, my primary responsibility is to represent in artistic form a given company's brand identity, not my own. I bring all my expertise and skill to bear in the process, but I check my ego at the door.

Even when I sign my work, I like to do so in a discreet way. I might hide it somewhere within the borders of the composition or match it to the style of the piece so it blends in seamlessly. Regrettably, I wasn't always this way. In high school and college, I would always sign my art pieces with a big, messy signature in the corner of the page like I was signing a football jersey. I look back at those pieces and just shake my head. Nothing can ruin a good composition like a grandiose John Hancock of a signature.

It often feels strange to mitigate so much of my own effect from the creation when I am the creator. The way I reconcile this paradox is by thinking of the artistic process in terms of surgery. Before entering the operating room, the doctor will scrub up for several minutes and be dressed head to toe in sterile garb so as not to contaminate the patient. Furthermore, the mark of a good surgeon is the lack of marks. A surgeon earns their renown by sewing up their incisions in a way that leaves little to no scars. Nobody would want a surgeon who likes to express themself by their creative take on surgery or who signs their name on your gallbladder before stitching you back up.

However, there are times when investing more of myself is exactly what the piece calls for. Allowing my heart, my pain, my passion—in a nutshell, my own humanity—to shine through can add a new level of depth and brilliance. Such is the case on my current sculpture of a bear. I have spent more than a year and a half on the carving of the Richardson family crest, and I have come to the figure of a grizzly raised up on its hind legs on the right side of the shield. In heraldic tradition, the bear is the symbol of protection of family. In the case of this crest, I chose it to represent protection of the Richardson family, the family of Christ, and the institution of family as ordained by God.

Each portion of the crest up to this point has required every ounce of my skill and then some. I have poured myself out for the sake of this one sculpture many times over. But I am ever aware that this piece is ultimately meant for the Richardson family and their successive generations. To be commissioned for such a work is an honor of a lifetime; to be entrusted with their family legacy is a responsibility of the ages. Up to this point I have been like the surgeon: I'm careful not to contaminate the piece with my own personal narrative.

But something shifted in me when it came time to carve the bear. As I told some spiritual mentors of mine, I felt compelled to live into the piece more fully. In doing so, I thought it might help me refocus my efforts by being more emotionally attached and drawn into the meaning of the symbols. When I wrote that in an email to these dear souls, I hardly knew at the time what I meant by it. It is now forever earmarked as one of those occasions in my life when I believe God was speaking *to me, through me* in a way only He can. I had no idea what trial was about to befall my family or how I would be called to defend it.

A Family Man

I genuinely feel mine is a life blessed beyond measure. I have a beautiful wife who is my best friend and soulmate. She has given me four beautiful children who I absolutely adore. I am a family man through and through. I have dreamed of having a large cackle of kids myself since I was just a boy. My version of ecstasy involves kiddos piled on top of me in the middle of our family room floor after a raucous tickle fight. Or being snuggled up in our king-size bed together beneath a set of six-foot wings I carved to represent the protection of God. I still remember carving those wings as a younger man while engaged to Hannah. I would daydream between chisel blows about what blessings of God they would bear witness to as our burgeoning family grew and grew. Today I am living that dream.

I would go to the ends of the earth for the sake of my wife and kids and fight tooth and nail for them. Well, my journey to earth's end is currently afoot, and my fight is here.

A Dark Day

Our oldest daughter, Emma, started having some interesting symptoms around the start of spring this year. Little things, ordinary kid things, like a skin rash that started showing up on her face, knees, and elbows. Being fairly well-practiced parents, four kids in at this point, we were not at all in a panic. Perhaps at the dawn of our parenting career, when we were green to the oddities of childhood changes, we might have sounded the alarm. In those days, a shift in the color of their boogers or a splinter in their finger was cause enough to ring the doctor. But eight years along and four souls deep, a skin rash was hardly a blip on our radar. A little ointment and she was back on her way.

Adding to it, our youngest, Eleanor, was born right around the same time Emma started showing some of these innocuous symptoms, so there was plenty of excitement and weariness to keep us occupied.

However, despite the regular lubing, the rash persisted and new changes, subtle as they were, began to appear. Emma was pulling herself out of play with other kids and sitting with the adults. We thought it was maybe just a sign of her early maturity and introverted temperament. But then she started losing weight and complaining about pain in her feet and hands. She was having trouble going up and down the stairs. Watching her walk or try to run was painful. So we eventually did make that call to the doctor.

The day came when her blood work arrived. Emma's charts showed her white blood cell count was very low, and many of her other levels were outside of normal range. All of a sudden our confidence as well-seasoned parents melted away, and we were like deer in the headlights, stunned by blinding worry once again.

My impulse after reading the blood work with Hannah was to find Emma. I wanted to see her. I wanted to be near her. I wanted to hold her close and tell her everything was going to be okay. The truth of the matter was, she had no idea of the apparent danger she was in. And for the moment, my responsibility as her father was to capture her in her glorious innocence and maintain her peace of mind. Telling her that she would be all right would only alarm her of the fact that she was *not all right.* Still, I had to be with her, if not for her sake, then for my own.

It was late in the day and I found her sitting alone up in one of our plastic patio chairs in the playhouse at the edge of our property. I climbed the worn-out cedar ladder, which groaned under my adult-sized footsteps. I stooped beneath the low-slatted ceiling and sat in the chair next to her. After a hard swallow to push my heart out of my throat, I said, "Hey kiddo . . . how are you doing?" Without lifting her tired gaze from the wildflower garden below, she simply replied, "Good."

I was seeing Emma in a new light at that moment. It was as if the blood test had revealed what we were too fearful to see: Our baby girl was sick and diminished. She looked frail and tired in that evening light—the bright orange bandage from her blood draw still wrapped around her skinny arm. I did not want to alarm her to the potential grievousness of her health—because the truth of the matter was I didn't even know . . . not fully anyway. However, at the same time she knew something wasn't quite right. I told her how brave I thought she was for getting her blood drawn. I told her that Mommy, Daddy, and the doctors were working to get her well and find the right medicine to get the pain in her hands and feet to go away. She replied, "But there's no pain in heaven, right?" In my nervous and tender state, that response caught me off guard. It poked at the very worst fear in the back of my mind. I had to turn my head for a moment, pretending something had caught my attention, before I gulped my heart back down again and said, "Yeah, sweetie . . . there is no pain in heaven. But we are going to work so you have less pain now."

That day began three of the most fraught weeks of my life.

Possible diagnoses of leukemia, lymphoma, or lupus were all on the table and haunted our minds unceasingly. Hannah and I sent out "prayer flares," as we call them, to our close friends and family to alert them of our situation. We pleaded to the Lord for help quite literally day and night. For a week straight at least, I would wake up at three o'clock in the morning on the dot every night. I would lay awake and think and pray. Many nights I went and crawled in bed with Emma and held her. Fear had turned my world upside down; my kids were supposed to come crawl in bed with me when they got scared, not the other way around.

And of course I had to keep working. I had deadlines looming, including this book. With the medical bills already piling up and more to come, I had to somehow maintain business as usual. But work proved near impossible. I could not focus to save my life. Even the most thrilling aspects of my work could not draw me into creative flow.

My heart found a new resting rate at double its normal pace and remained there for days on end. I could not go more than half an hour working in the shop without poking my head in the door from the garage to see how Emma was feeling. Repeatedly, I had to force myself to get back to work.

Provoking the Beast

As many tears as woodchips fell to the carving studio floor during those tumultuous weeks. There were moments while chiseling away when I would burst into tears mid-stroke. I cried out to God every day, multiple times a day, for the sake of my precious baby girl. Either with my hands to the heavens or my face to the dusty floor, I prayed till I didn't know what to pray anymore. In the mighty name of Jesus, I shouted aloud against the work of the Enemy there in our enclosed garage. Fits of rage overtook me for the sake of my sweet daughter as I paced the length of my woodshop in puffs of anger—still clenching the mallet and chisel in my hands till my forearms burned and my knuckles turned white.

It was then and there that I chose to make a major change to the sculpture of the bear I was working on. In the initial drawing of the crest, the bear's mouth was agape but the face was relatively stoic. But now, as I was carving, I would make the bear forever wear my passion and rage. So I flared the nostrils of the beast and snarled its snout with anger. I furrowed its brow and filled his eyes with ferocity. I made the hair on its neck and shoulder stand on end. I widened the bear's mouth to reveal more of his glaring and sharpened teeth. I went as far as carving its gnarled tongue inside his mouth and the ridges in his upper pallet. His chest is billowed with a forthcoming roar. I chiseled him as a gargoyle of my righteous fatherly anger.

Emma's primary care doctor told us it would take three to six months to get in to see the specialists that we needed to. I wouldn't stand for it. The first two weeks were a living hell, and I could not imagine enduring additional months of the same. What is more, how could I just sit back and wait while my daughter diminished further? Absolutely not! Getting seen and getting real answers became my fight.

I was calling everyone I knew for favors, advice, and possible connections. God did hear my roars of prayer. What was supposed to take months to get Emma in to see a specialist happened over the course of a week. Our neurologist neighbor and precious friend got us connected with a hematologist (blood and cancer specialist) who saw us the very next day and helped us rule out cancer. I fell to tears and hugged the doctor when she told us. The hematologist said this seemed more rheumatological.

The day after that, it was my cousin-in-law—a rheumatologist now living on the East Coast—who was able to give a possible diagnosis via Emma's blood work, symptom list, and pictures. He then referred us to the rheumatology department at the children's hospital where he had done his fellowship. We got in there two days after that.

The doctors at the hospital concurred with my cousin's diagnosis: juvenile dermatomyositis, or JDM. It is a very rare but treatable (praise the Lord!) autoimmune disease. We have only just begun Emma's treatment, and we have a long road ahead, but I am glad to report she is already showing improvement. She has a 30 percent chance of growing out of it and never contending with it again, which is now our new fight and our unceasing prayer.

I have been able to pick up the pace again on my work, and the bear with his permanent scowl is nearly finished. He will find his place in the overall composition of the crest and stand boldly as a symbol of familial protection for ages to come. But to me he is a monument of my personal battle for my own family.

Yes, this piece is not mine in the end, but I have taken the liberty as its creator to make it in my image. The bear, in a sense, is my own self-portrait at the time that I created it. All my passion and protectiveness, all my angst and anger, all my torment and fear are carved and crystallized in the form of that fomenting, ferocious beast. And why shouldn't it be so? This symbol of protection of family has been made more powerful and more authentic by the investiture of this man's love for his daughter. The fight in the bear is my fight for Emma. Its teeth and claws are mine bared at her illness and enemies. And its thunderous roar is my prayer, like the Spirit's over all of us—groanings too deep for words.

While our hand and our head may be all that is required for some acts of creation, the pouring out of our hearts for others can transform and elevate the nature of our work and us with it. The revelation of our maker's heart to the world also reveals the Maker's heart in us, through us, and for us. If I, an earthly father, cry and fight and roar in prayer for the sake of my children, how much more does your Father in heaven cry and fight and roar in groanings too deep for words over you? God broods like a great bear in jealous love over you, and the rumbles of His mighty roar can shake the very foundations of hell for your sake.

From My Heart to Yours

If you were to observe my life through the keyhole of social media, you might think I live in an enchanted world untouched by trouble, but that is hardly the full picture. As an artist, I have set sail on the seas of trouble. I live a topsy-turvy existence that few, I think, would have the stomach for. The very nature of my career and calling requires a great deal of faith to keep me afloat. But rough seas make good sailors. And what is more, I keep a tight ship. I know where my true priorities lie and what is most important. Not to mention, I never go sailing without the One who commands the winds and the waves.

If you are going through a trial like mine, please know that my heart and all the prayers from it are with you. I always mistook that line from C. S. Lewis in his *The Problem of Pain*, where he says, "God whispers to us in our pleasures, speaks in our conscience, but shouts in our pain: it is His megaphone to rouse a deaf world."[1] For whatever reason, I mistook it to mean that God shouts *at us*. But that is not true, and that is not what Lewis wrote. Having just come through a great pain, and still in it to a great degree, I can tell you He does indeed shout *to us*, and what He is shouting is, "*I am here and*

I am with you!" He not only shouts to us but shouts *with us* against the oncoming darkness.

The Grit in My Paint

You might not have expected this sort of thing in a book on making and creativity, but the lesson here is I do not create in a vacuum—and neither does anyone else. I can no sooner escape the trials of this world when I create than I can defy the bonds of gravity. Reality finds you where you are at. Being able to compartmentalize is often the right and healthy thing to do. Not letting pain or grief rule over every aspect of your life takes a great deal of spiritual wisdom and stamina.

I DO NOT CREATE IN A VACUUM—AND NEITHER DOES ANYONE ELSE.

But occasionally, there are times when you should open the floodgates of your heart and let your life be awash in exactly what it is that the Lord is teaching you at that time. Take your grief and put it to work. Gather your own shattered pieces and turn misfortune into a mosaic. Build an Ebenezer to the Lord of the stones life throws at you. I cannot give you any set formula on how to do so. I can only open you up to the idea. The possibilities are too numerous and applications too specific. What I can say is, lean into the Lord. He is the real master of this art form, after all. The maker's heart in you is His heart. He takes what the Enemy intends for evil and turns it for good. If there is one technique of creation I would like to learn from God, this would be it. And the best way to learn is by imitating.

CHAPTER THIRTEEN

FEAST AND FAMINE

Finding Financial Stability

If you looked in the table of contents and saw this chapter listed, your response might have been, "An *artist* talking about finances? You've got to be kidding me!" If so, I am right there with you! No one is more surprised than me that I have decided to broach this topic. I am not a financial planner, guru, or savant, and I would never pretend to be. Nor am I independently wealthy. Despite how it might appear from the outside looking in, I am not "rolling in it." I have not struck it rich, though a guy can still dream now and then. I make a living from my art—not a killing.

I MAKE A LIVING FROM MY ART—NOT A KILLING.

The only reason I felt so compelled to include some commentary on this topic is because it is a question I am so often asked. I think people are impressed that I earn a living from my art on the same level as seeing a dog walk on its hind legs—it's not that I do it so well, but that I do it at all.

The stereotypical artist is a starving one. I've heard it a thousand times or more. Predictably, when I am introduced to someone new and I tell them what I do, often they respond, "Oh, one of those starving artists, right?!" That is when I want to shake their hand all the harder, stare deep into their eyes with a glare, and just say, "Famished!" If I am sitting next to them at dinner, I want to interrupt their meal at each course, glance down at their plate, and ask, "Are you going to finish that?" After all, if they have painted me in that box, who am I to disabuse them of their preconceptions? I only wish I were so snarky and bold . . . and then again, maybe not. By and by I just smile and don't say anything at all.

The truth of the matter is that I have been a starving artist at one point or another, so perhaps the stranger is right to some degree. Those days may be behind me, but they feel *right* behind me all the time. I might be sitting high on the hog for the moment, but in the back of my mind, I know it doesn't always last. Feast and famine come as regular seasons in my line of work. You learn very quickly to ration the feast for the coming famine. In the end, it evens out to daily bread, to manna from heaven, and somehow there is always enough.

Therefore, whatever advice I dispense in this chapter is not prescriptive but descriptive. I think this way about life and business in general. Rarely, if ever, can you copy and paste the same business model or financial plan from one entity to another and expect the same results. There are far too many variables at play. Many of the breakthroughs in my career have come as dumb luck to some—more like God's blessings to me. I could no sooner convey to you my same successes than I could make lightning strike, though I would if I could, dear friend. Who knows! You might very well do far better than me in this arena, which is really not hard to do. Still, I humbly offer up what wisdom I have on this score.

While I can and will share with you some of the specifics of my business infrastructure, what I really want you to take away are lasting principles. I can stand by these principles with confidence because they are not my own; they are borrowed from those who are far wiser than me. These doctrines of finance are what helped me navigate the challenges of my industry and eventually got me walking on my hind legs.

The Holy Hustle

One of the reasons why artists are so bad at business is because we love what we do. The problem here is twofold. On the one hand, what we create feels inspired and sacred, so the involvement of dirty money seems to cheapen it even if the price is fair. An artist strives to imbue their work with surpassing intrinsic value. Assigning a dollar amount to it sucks the romantic air right out. Moreover, creating is an incredibly vulnerable act. A rejection on the basis of price is still a rejection. A particular shopper may just not have the budget for a given work of art, which in theory should not reflect on the value of the art piece, and especially not the self-worth of the artist. And yet it still does.

On the other hand, it feels awkward to ask for money for something we enjoy doing and would continue to do regardless of its profitability. The delight we take in our work is also the reason we underestimate *and* undervalue our time. Since I started my business, mentors of mine have implored me to track my hours to better gauge the profitability of a project. But when I create, I want time to melt away. I want to reach that point of flow where I am absolutely immersed in whatever it is that I am doing. As REM is a symptom of deep sleep, one of the telltale signs that I have reached flow is that I have lost all track of time. Putting myself "on the clock," therefore, feels counterproductive.

I do not think that the aforementioned characteristics are specific only to artists. I imagine these very human tendencies and the psychology behind them exist across a wide range of occupations. I have a friend who is a business consultant and entrepreneurial coach, and he also struggles with putting a price on his time, though he helps others through this struggle regularly.

You may also find valuing your time extremely difficult. The very idea might poke and prod at your many underlying insecurities as a maker. First, the fears swirl around the work itself: *What if no one buys what I am selling? What if they think my work is not worth the price I put on it? What if I tarnish this shining thing I've created with a price tag, a barcode, and dirty old money?* The fear seeps deeper still and begins to attack your heart like a virus: *What if people think I'm a grubby mercenary—that I'm in it only for the money? What if they are offended by the price of my work and they don't want anything to do with me anymore?* And the final blow: *What if I am just not good enough?* That deep-seated fear might be the very thing keeping you from bringing your talents and wares to market. You think, *Why do anything that might pose questions I'd rather not know the answer to?*

The real danger of letting this rule over you for long is that it will stop you from creating altogether. Sure, you might dabble privately, but you won't generate anything substantial enough that, God forfend, someone might inquire to buy and that awkward conversation you have been so adamantly avoiding finds you anyway. *No!* You think it is better to play it small or, perhaps, not at all. Listen to me: You can't let this hold you back! You need to be brave in this as in every other aspect of creating. What you make is too valuable in the world to let a silly thing like money stop you. And if I could whisper through the page, I would tell you to lean in closer for this one: The right customer, client, patron, or fan is not only able to pay you a fair price—they *want* to!

People often go on about not wanting relationships to be transactional—and neither do I. But nor do I see the money someone graciously pays me for my art as altogether unholy. On the contrary, it is *quite* holy. Money is merely the medium of value that simplifies the exchange, but those dollars and cents, mundane as they may seem, translate to miraculous provisions innumerable: It is the food that fills my kids' bellies; it is the medicine and hospital visits that help to heal them; it is the education that grows their minds; it is the roof and walls that hem us in; it is the heat that warms us and the water that bathes us; it is the light that shines on us all and on the work on my drawing table, where I return to perpetuate this miraculous exchange.

Like anything, learning to price your time and work takes practice. And while it may never be altogether easy, it does get *easier*. Doing a bit of research and finding at what price others offer a similar product can serve as a benchmark to help you determine fair market value of your services, output, and time. When you eventually do sell something, you set a precedent to point back to for the next time. Having even one transaction under your belt makes the subsequent sales all the easier. You will likely increase that price little by little over time, but at least you have a starting point. Eventually, it will be less and less of a struggle, and those fears you had before will fade over time.

While I still struggle with pricing my work even thirteen years into business, I have certainly gotten better at what we call the "Holy Hustle." Hannah and I casually coined this term some years ago to help me rectify the dual nature of our work as both *sacred* and *sellable*.

On the one hand, the work itself is an act of devotion born out of countless holy moments inside a sacred studio. On the other hand, it is a product to be sold. It can feel jarring for the piece to undergo such a categorical transformation in our minds. We like to think of creating art pieces like raising kids: You bring them up right, you try to pour your very best into them, but eventually, they must leave home and get a job. Holding on to art pieces, like holding on to kids, is counterproductive and very expensive.

The sale of those art pieces is what feeds our actual offspring, and that is holy. And for that righteous cause, we are willing to do anything.

Fiscal Feedback

One of the earliest opportunities I was given to sell my art on a professional level was working for a couple of different clothing companies in Los Angeles while I was going to school out there. A friend of mine in college was an art student at Biola University and had a part-time job as a graphic designer for a clothing company in Orange County. He had seen my drawings and the script calligraphy I was just learning at the time. He thought the owners of the company would like to see what I was doing and possibly hire me to do some T-shirt designs. It was the early 2000s and graphic tees were all the rage. Companies like RVCA, Affliction, and Ed Hardy were setting the trend.

When I met with the owners of the clothing company and showed them my rather humble portfolio, they were ecstatic. We started brainstorming ideas right on the spot. They had a really good bead on the market. Knowing what was trending and what would sell, they gave some great themes to explore without being too didactic. I left the meeting anxious to get started on their shopping list of ideas.

That introduction marked the beginning of a great new outlet for my art. I produced many T-shirt designs that sold through Nordstrom, Urban Outfitters, and many other retailers around the country. I loved the direct feedback I received from the company owners. They would tell me how good or bad a certain T-shirt design performed based on the number of orders placed by retailers. Over time, I was able to anticipate trends and generate new designs on my own. I would bring my latest drawings to the owners, and they would freak out. After my designs were launched as a part of their next season's line, they would give me a letter grade on how well they were received by their buyers. I thoroughly enjoyed this process. I was not only working a real job as an artist but also testing out my burgeoning style in the real world. Being so far removed from consumers but still seeing the numbers gave me the opportunity to read the receptibility of my artwork by that metric alone. It might have been less personal, but there is great value when the market speaks.

What that first job in T-shirt design taught me was that commerce can actually be a fantastic form of feedback. Graphic tees may not exactly rise to the level of high art, but producing designs with broad enough appeal to sell in bulk to major retailers grew me as a fine artist. Anticipating the wishes of the end buyer and trying to anticipate what someone would be willing to pay for and clothe themselves with got me out of my own head. I was exploring new themes and concepts that I never would have on my own. Just as a good chef tastes everything to expand their palate, I was exploring more and more concepts, and it was a boon to my creativity.

One time the art director at the clothing company asked me to include a skull in my next composition. With the designs of old tattoo artists like Sailor Jerry and Ed Hardy making a big resurgence, people could not get enough of skulls. I rolled my eyes at this initially. I thought skulls were overused, unoriginal, and done for cheap shock value. But the challenge that drew me in was how to approach the skull in a new and original way. And to further challenge myself, maybe I could represent that gothic icon in a sophisticated way. I was getting my degree in psychology at the time, so I wanted to explore the subconscious fixation on skulls. I came to the realization that the skull is the face of our own mortality. So I collected song lyrics, poetry verses, and famous quotes about death and wrote them all in beautiful script with white ink on black paper in the form of a skull. The contrast of that typically hard image composed of soft, flowing script made the image so dynamic. There was still some of that shock value that people obviously know and crave, but it was tempered by those flourished words. And not just any words, but man's reflection on his mortality transcribed in the face of his mortality. They sold by the bushel!

If you are generally repellent to the idea of money and regard it merely as a necessary evil, think of how else that transactional interchange between you and your customer or client can inform your craft and serve the relationship. Beyond keeping the lights on, consider what else there is to glean and gain from that facet of your vocation. It will not only help you take a more holistic approach to your business but may also serve to redeem the indigestion that money matters often cause. Who knows, you might be able to look into the face of something that scares you and discover some poetry there.

Especially in my online business, I depend heavily on this metric of feedback, as I am not able to see the vast majority of my customers face-to-face. In person, I can read facial expressions, tone, and body language. I can enter into a conversation and discover if the piece and the message behind it came through to them. But when there is a World Wide Web between us, often all I have to go on is if they made the purchase or not. In many respects, it is one of the most honest forms of feedback I receive. I might earn glowing reviews and lavish praise from family, friends, or followers over a new art piece, but if nobody actually buys it, I know I have missed the mark somehow. I don't let it get me down. It is matter-of-fact and is more kind than someone actually voicing their discontent.

I know this might seem trite, like I am playing to the crowd. But what is the alternative? Creating just for myself? A postmodernist or a professor in the echo chamber of academia might reply yes. But in my mind, that is not at all what it means to be an effective artist. A good artist may have a well-developed voice of their own, while a great artist is the voice of those around them. If you do not listen to those around you, how can you ever expect to be their voice, to speak to what is on their heart? To put into words what they themselves cannot articulate. To put into pictures, song, or dance what cannot be said in words. Money may feel like background noise convoluting the creative process, but it is actually another prime opportunity to listen.

MONEY MAY FEEL LIKE BACKGROUND NOISE CONVOLUTING THE CREATIVE PROCESS, BUT IT IS ACTUALLY ANOTHER PRIME OPPORTUNITY TO LISTEN.

Famine

I experienced my first famine within year one of our marriage. That line of our vows—for richer, for poorer—was immediately put to the test. Commissions and print sales were meager at best. I was sequestered to create a large commission piece but soon realized it came with a massive opportunity cost. I had also shelled out nearly ten thousand dollars for a custom-made website that always glitched on the user at the moment of checkout. I'm pretty sure I paid extra for that. Cash flow being what it was meant that I had to let go of the one employee I had—a friend of mine who had only come on a few months earlier. I also fired my wife, which I think really put the cherry on top of our nuptials. I've always said firing her was an act of self-preservation: Either I fired her or she was going to kill me. So there I was, flying solo once again, trying to patch up my infrastructure, keep the books, ship orders, grow my portfolio, and just occasionally sell some art.

The only thing really keeping me afloat at the time was the single commission and the regular sale of my handmade calligraphy pens. I was still making art, of course, and listing my prints for sale on my lemonade stand of a website, but I had few takers. Who knows? I might have had more, but my website was rejecting transactions with such regularity that it seemed the feature, not the bug.

My brother, Josh, and his friend Mike, a website designer, took pity on me. Without even consulting me first, they built me an entirely new website on a simple Shopify platform. They both asked to meet me at a coffee shop without telling me why. The whole setup felt like an intervention, and to some degree I guess it was. I was at my wits' end trying to make my overly expensive, tailor-made website work. I paid for bespoke, but what I got was broke. Remember in the pentimento chapter where I said, "You shouldn't hold on to a mistake just because you spent a lot of time making it"? Well, here I would adapt that phrase: Don't hold on to a mistake just because you paid a lot for it.

At a small table in the corner of the coffee shop my intervention came. Josh and Mike sat down and told me what I already knew—my website was a dumpster fire. It is one thing to know you have a problem, but when someone comes to you unprompted and flat out says so, it brings you to a whole new level of awareness.

DON'T HOLD ON TO A MISTAKE JUST BECAUSE YOU PAID A LOT FOR IT.

Josh explained how they had each taken some time out of their schedule to voluntarily build me a whole new site. They copied and pasted what they could as far as pictures and text from my URL and plugged it into a template. As my brother, Josh knew my aesthetic well enough to act as the designer, and Mike did all the building. Mike had his laptop on the table but kept the screen facing him while they laid out all they had done. Finally, they turned the screen around.

I was in disbelief for several minutes as they seamlessly navigated through page after page of an intuitive site map. Every one of my art images loaded quickly. Every link worked. They even took me through the checkout process, and wouldn't you know it, the transaction completed without a hitch. There were still some edits to make and content to add, but it was worlds better than my custom screw-up of a website.

After their walk-through of the new site, they said something to the effect of, "Jake, you can keep trying to make your current website work, or you can take this one. Either way, our feelings won't be hurt. We just want to help you." I sat there staring at the screen for several moments. It was like being on a sinking ship I had been bailing water out of for months. And along comes someone with a brand-new boat who bids me, "Come aboard!"

The new website was a massive change, and I felt like I had a new lease on business. The orders did not come flooding in, however. They may have ticked up a little bit, and very quickly my customers were praising the new site. But for the time being, I remained a starving artist.

The Feast

A couple of months went by and business was as slow as usual. I had a standing meeting with one of my mentors to look over the books and discuss new strategies. After running through the numbers on another sad quarter, I asked Steve, "What can I do to help the situation?"

Steve gave a small shrug and said, "Keep stocking the pond!"

I responded rather passionately: "Steve, I am stocking the pond! The pond is stocked, but no one is fishing!"

The one glimmer of hope at the time was a micro documentary sponsored by Coors that I was featured in that was scheduled to air. We had shot the piece on my work several months before. While I poured my heart into that project and created a special title piece, *Craftsmanship*, just for the affair, I was honestly not expecting much of it.

I opened the email from the production company and clicked on the link. The micro documentary had turned out far better than we imagined. It had involved two grueling days of shooting and two weeks of prep work and art creation, all distilled down to five minutes. The production company had done us proud—they were the best five minutes and edited beautifully.

As impressed as we were with the outcome, we never could've imagined how it would be received over that coming week. Within the first twenty-four hours it had racked up more than a hundred thousand views. In less than a week they had gotten more than twenty million views on their site, UPROXX, and another five million views on YouTube. It was my first experience going viral.

I now had a different problem. My proverbial "stocked pond" was running low. The surge of attention brought people to my website in droves. I was now more thankful than ever that I had made the switch to a new website only weeks earlier. I shivered to think of the revenue I might have lost had I stuck with my earlier broken version. I was receiving so many orders that the guy making my prints could not keep up. I had to sequester two other fine art printers just to meet the demand.

Hannah came back to work for me full-time. She was helping me get prints signed, packaged, and off to the post office. The *cha-ching* of an old cash register was our notification of each sale on our website. At one point, with uncanny regularity, for every print we finished packaging . . . *cha-ching!* . . . another print was sold. This went on for several hours. It seemed impossible to keep up, and we were thrilled out of our minds!

Late in the week we got a call from a number I didn't recognize. I picked up the phone and the woman on the other end introduced herself and told me she had a client who was desperate to get in touch with me. She went on to say that she had sent some documents to my email and I needed to sign them and get them back to her so that she could connect me with her client ASAP. She beseeched me that time was of the essence and would say no more.

This felt a little scammy at the time, so we proceeded with caution. I went to my inbox right away, found her email, and downloaded the attached document. The letterhead read "Apple Inc."

Certainly this could not be that *Apple*, I thought. I signed the document, returned it to her, and called her back. She told me to hang on the line and she would three-way in her client. An executive with Apple came on the line and explained how they had seen my work and wanted to contract me for a special project. The only thing was I would have to fly out to California in two days. I asked what the project was and he replied, "Unfortunately, I can't tell you that." He explained that this was a black project and he would compensate me for my time, which would likely be about a week, and to pack accordingly. It all felt very cloak and dagger, but what was I gonna do, say no to Apple? So, I blindly agreed. He said his staff would be in touch shortly to make all the arrangements.

What on earth is happening? I thought at the time. Surely Apple had done enough research to know that I worked with a *dip pen*! What could the largest technology company in the world want with me—an analog artist? I imagined the whole arrangement falling apart once they discovered I had no technological experience. Perhaps they wanted me to do some logo design or consult with their graphics department on a new typeface. My mind was reeling with the possibilities.

Two days later, a black limousine pulled up in front of my condo to take Hannah and me to the airport. Apple had booked us first-class seats. Hannah had very little flying experience up to that point whereas I had done a fair bit of traveling but always in coach. We were both giddy with excitement, but I leaned over to her and said quietly, "Don't get used to this. You married an artist, after all."

When we landed at LAX and made our way down to baggage claim, a chauffeur complete with a suit and black cap was holding up a sign with my name on it. It felt like I was in a scene out of the movies, which seemed fitting for Tinseltown. That limousine drove us to a luxury hotel in West Hollywood, where we were booked into a suite.

Communication came the next day via text that I was to meet the executive and his team in a different room in the same hotel. When I knocked on the door of the room, a security guard in a suit with an earpiece greeted me at the door.

Inside sat a small group of people, some looking as nervous as I felt. I was ushered into the middle of the room to sit in a swanky, white leather C-shaped couch with a few other guys—the nervous ones. Before we were all introduced, the tall bloke who had answered the door asked us to surrender our phones and gave us a long lecture about not posting or sharing anything from the day. He told us that security would be monitoring all our social media pages, and if anything regarding the project or our involvement was shared, we would be immediately ejected from the project and charges may be filed against us. He concluded his little speech with a simple "Thank you." *Thank you for what?* I thought. Thank you for being scared out of our minds? Thank you for not soiling ourselves on the white couch after your terrifying speech?

At length, the executive who I had talked to on the phone stepped forward and introduced himself. He addressed those of us in the C-shaped hot seats as a select group of artists chosen from around the world to play a unique role in this project. He told us he had some very exciting new devices that we would be working with over the next week.

Our attention was diverted to what looked like a large gun safe in the corner of the room, and there another man was fiddling with the combination knob. He unlatched the large steel door and brought out a stack of black cases. The executive took one of the black cases, opened it, and pulled out an iPad Pro with an Apple Pencil—the very first of their kind.

Our assignment, if we chose to accept it, was to create an original work of art in our respective style using the iPad Pro and the

Apple Pencil over the next three days. We would then be featured with our art pieces in a promo video at the end of the week.

The Apple executive then introduced the engineer and the designer of the app Procreate and said they were there to help us get started.

The designer went artist by artist, showing us which brush tool to use within the app. When they came to me, they said they had designed a special calligraphy brush tool for me to use and had me try it out right there on the spot. It was all wrong! It was sort of shaped like the end of a broad-edged pen but twisted wildly when you wrote with it. I would not be able to use it at all. I got a sick feeling in the pit of my stomach and thought I might have to excuse myself from this whole thing. Then it occurred to me that in my backpack I had one of my calligraphy pens and an inkwell. Not knowing exactly what I was getting into, I had packed everything. I told the engineer and designer that I had a dip pen and could show them how it worked. Then maybe they could design a brush profile that simulated the real thing. I was stabbing in the dark and hoping beyond hope that I could remedy this situation and fast. I set up shop on a small section of desk space next to a slew of laptops. With pen in hand, I had a room of computer geniuses and Apple executives clamoring around me. It was a surreal moment!

I gave a crash course on my antique writing tool to the creators of Procreate. I had them sit and write with it and feel the action of the pen nib on the paper. You could almost see the light bulbs flashing above their heads as they started writing code and talking back and forth about what parameters needed changing and what the sensitivity levels needed to be set at. It wasn't more than fifteen minutes later that they handed the iPad back to me and said, "Try this!" The moment I put the Apple Pencil to the screen, that foreign tool felt immediately familiar in my hand. It responded beautifully to the pressure of my fingertips in much the same way a real pen did. I looked up from the screen with a smile and said, "This will work!"

That entire week was a blur. I had to familiarize myself with the iPad, create an art piece, go to wardrobe to get outfitted, and perform my art for the camera.

The set was in a legitimate Hollywood film studio. I guess someone from set design read in my bio that I was from Colorado, for the stage was set like a posh art studio with a backdrop of aspen trees through the glass doors behind me. A massive camera was set on rails in front of the desk where I would be working. It had a lens on it like something out of a Dr. Seuss book—like a giant telescope turned backward that tapered down to a very small end the size of a toilet paper roll.

I sat down at the desk and the iPad Pro with an earlier version of my art already cued up and loaded on the screen. The prop master came by to give the screen one last wipe. From behind the glowing veil of the lights, I could faintly see the director sitting in his canvas folding chair. He asked if I was ready and I replied, "Yes, sir!" Several calls rang out: "Quiet on the set! . . . Speed . . . Action!" My heart was pounding but my hand was steady. Cradling the Apple Pencil in my fingers, I hovered over the screen and touched down in motion to perform a long, falling figure eight flourish. In my periphery I could see the eye of the Dr. Seuss lens following my every move. I paused only for a moment and was about to lay down another stroke when I heard, "Cut!" The director got up out of his chair and marched straight toward me. For a moment I thought I had totally messed up, even though everything felt right. "That was unbelievable!" I heard the director exclaim. "That stroke was absolutely lyrical! You have the steadiest hand of anyone we have shot yet. Do it again!"

The rest is history, as they say. I was asked several more times to work with Apple over the coming months. They invited me to their special event for the unveiling of the iPad Pro and the Apple Pencil, where I got to see the finished promo video for the very first time. My art piece was featured on the big screen as part of the presentation of the Apple Pencil.

Each time I worked with Apple, Hannah and I were treated like royalty and flown out first class. On one trip, Hannah turned to me and raised her complimentary glass of champagne in her reclined leather seat and said, "Not getting used to it!"

From a five-minute video came a seemingly everlasting feast. It has been ten years to the month as I write this since that all transpired, and I can still trace many of the dominoes that fell in my career from that day to this. I had a slew of other opportunities that I could not have dreamed of. I was asked to speak at Pixar Studios to a group of animators; I was featured on a PBS show, *A Craftsman's Legacy*; and I've had many features in newspapers, magazines, and online profiles.

That particular feast did eventually wane, as all feasts do. My website has never *cha-chinged* with the same regularity as it did during those wild days of virality. I am not getting calls from big tech companies or being filmed in Hollywood studios. I have returned to a quiet life of working with my hands. Other feasts have come over the years, but no two have ever looked the same.

The important lesson I have learned through lavish and lean times is to ration the feast for the coming famine. While there have been many occasions when it feels like my ship has finally come in—at long last I have been discovered and the days of being a starving artist are behind me!—reality tells a far more complex story. Financial performance graphed over the course of my career may show a trend line moving gradually up and to the right, but there are several points scattered above and below that line. I have learned not to count on the high ones or fear the low ones.

Not counting on the high points means that I do not automatically adjust my lifestyle and spending to match the plentitude of that moment. I may make some reasonable investments in inventory or tools while cash flow is up, but I don't go on a wild spending spree. Immediately, I sock away a large portion of it in our business savings account in anticipation of end-of-the-year expenses—for the ones I can foresee, and a little extra for the ones I can't.

THE IMPORTANT LESSON I HAVE LEARNED THROUGH LAVISH AND LEAN TIMES IS TO RATION THE FEAST FOR THE COMING FAMINE.

I also do not fear the low points because (1) I have anticipated and prepared for them by stocking my storehouses, and (2) I use them to motivate me to kick it into high gear. Financial pressure holds my hands to the grindstone, and my productivity is thus increased out of sheer necessity. I have learned the seasonal ebb and flow of my business the same way a race car driver learns the track he is on. I know which months are the tight corners where my momentum will be slowed and our margins will be tight. Likewise, I can anticipate the straightaways like November to December when people are doing a lot of their Christmas shopping, and that is when I shift it into high gear and mash the gas pedal.

Gratitude

Human nature has convinced us that the grass is always greener on the other side of the hill. Social media shows us not the greenest sides but the *greenest patches* on countless hills the world over. We edit our lives down to the most favorable bits, water them thoroughly, trim them up nicely, and frame them in a shining white picket fence. Algorithms further weed out the picking to spotlight better hills and gardens than yours. If all we are shown are fertile patches of turf on what are otherwise desolate hills, is it any wonder that most of us live in a constant state of delusion and discontentment? Better we should turn our attention to our own hill, knock down our fences, overseed the barren ground, and irrigate it thoroughly. As my wife is fond of saying, "The grass is greener where you water it."

Perhaps one of the best ways to cultivate contentment in your life is by tapping into the wellspring of gratitude that flows from the heart of the maker.

One thing that living through regular famines will teach you is how to be grateful. I was talking with a friend of mine who is a software engineer. He had worked for some of the biggest tech companies on the planet and had lived a life of plenty. However, he had given up that life to rough it as a small-time entrepreneur. He is a man of deep and abiding faith and has said that one of the reasons he stepped out of the rat race was due in part to the fact that his regular and sizable income had made him more dependent on money and less reliant on God—something that is easy to do in the tech world. *Well! In my profession, a reliance on God is already baked into the cake!* That might seem like

ONE OF THE BEST WAYS TO CULTIVATE CONTENTMENT IN YOUR LIFE IS BY TAPPING INTO THE WELLSPRING OF GRATITUDE THAT FLOWS FROM THE HEART OF THE MAKER.

some sort of sad consolation prize from a life of irregular provision, but my friend's perspective really got me thinking.

Gratitude is the greatest elixir for countering discontentment and pride, which goes straight to the heart of the maker.

Generosity

There is perhaps no one I know who is more generous in their giving than my own wife. Yes, I know others who have given extravagantly, but they give out of their own extravagance. When I say that Hannah is one of the most generous people I know, it is because she gives out of her own scarcity. Part of the reason I can say she is the chief among givers is because I know her giving firsthand. After all, we share the same bank accounts. And the things she loves to give away most of all are the jewelry pieces we have created together at Everyday Heirloom Co. I have reminded her that when she gives away jewelry, it is different from giving away a book or an art print, or even cash for that matter, because what she is giving away is hard currency—actual silver and gold.

Up to this point, Hannah has given away thousands of dollars in jewelry. If you adjust that amount to reflect the current sky-high price of gold, it is thousands more and rising. She has given them to dear friends and perfect strangers. While some have been given in the name of marketing, most are simply a random act of gratis.

Her favorite way to gift her adornments is to take them directly off her own neck, wrist, or finger and put it on an unsuspecting person whom she has just met. She always listens to the Spirit of God to tell her just who and when, and she handles the rest. I have witnessed her do this dozens of times. The blessed recipient is almost always overwhelmed to tears by both the gift and the giver. There is something so powerful about the preciousness of the gift and the poignancy of its timing. I also think there is something in that gesture of Hannah giving something directly off her person—even more than if it were neatly boxed and gift wrapped. It speaks to the recipient in such a powerful and deeply personal level.

In full transparency, I've cringed a lot of the times Hannah has flung her gold and jewels before the masses. I think about how we will be further in the red with another month of negative cash flow. I think of the casting cost, the finishing cost, and the cost of my time to make it in the first place. I have all but stopped making Hannah jewelry for birthdays or anniversaries because she just ends up giving those away too. Only if I engrave them with something that is specific only to her, like her name or monogram, can I be sure that it stays around her neck or finger.

But each time the calculator pops up in my mind as I do my sums on Hannah's lavish giving, I am eventually if not immediately humbled. Hannah will fill me in about the harrowing story of a struggling widow raising her three kids on her own whom she just gave a necklace to, and I am put in my place.

One time at an art show, the barista who was working the coffee cart was perusing the art with tears running down her cheeks. Hannah fell into a deep conversation with her and, like clockwork, pulled a necklace from our display and placed it around her neck. Did she select the less expensive silver version? No, of course not! She took the ten-karat yellow gold one and strung it around her neck. She also grabbed the letter-pressed card from the display with her explanation of the piece and gave that to her as well.

Late that night after we got home from the event, Hannah received a text from that barista. She explained that she read the card for the necklace and was surprised to find that the design was based on 2 Corinthians 4:8–9. It just so happened to be her life verse and one of the first she had learned as a little girl. To her, that necklace and the message it carried was a wink from God.

In strictly financial terms, that event was an utter failure. But the opportunity to speak into that woman's life at a moment when she desperately needed it was of far greater value than what can be measured in dollars, cents, or even pure gold.

Jacques Maritain, in his book *The Responsibility of the Artist*, claims that the first act of the artist is gratis—the free gift of beauty.[1] In this way Maritain explains that the artist readily exemplifies the free gift of grace that was given to us through Jesus on the cross. Artists should therefore always lead in generosity and, in so doing, manifest the spirit of Christ.

Last One for the Tip Jar

Finances may always be something of a thorn in my side. But I will not let it keep me from striving to get better at stewarding what I have so that I can be even more effective in my business and generous in my giving. I am grateful for every morsel from heaven that feeds not only me but the mouths of my beloved. Am I a starving artist? Yes! But let my hunger be ever for the Lord. May I always have an insatiable appetite for God's presence that I find regularly in my work. Manna is an acquired taste, to be sure. But oh, how my spiritual palate craves it! And not merely for the void that it fills, but every bite is richly seasoned with the goodness of God. Each delightful morsel has the supernatural power to nourish heart, body, and soul. So let the stranger assume that I am a starving artist, for they assume rightly—and they shall never be able to fathom the depths of my appetite for God's sufficient grace!

And to you, dear reader, I pray that you always see God's

DO NOT LET THE HUSTLE OF MAKING MONEY SPOIL THE HOLINESS OF WHAT YOU MAKE.

hand of provision in your life—even through the leanest of times. Do not let the hustle of making money spoil the holiness of what you make. There will be times of famine and times of feasting as well, but always keep your maker's heart after His in a posture of gratitude.

CHAPTER FOURTEEN

SUPPORTERS

The Art of Relationship

If there is one thing I have learned over the course of my career, it is that true wealth comes not through my hands but through relationships. Whether in the form of partners, collaborators, mentors, patrons, advocates, or collectors, not all that glitters is gold. If you want to tap into treasures untold, learn to love others well and, what is often more challenging, let others love you.

Not a superficial kind of love, which you may receive from

fans or followers online. While I regularly receive a lot of genuine engagement from my followers, and some have even grown into true relationships, by and large social media is programmed for flattery as well as envy. But the sort of love I am talking about comes from people who know you well and like you anyway, as a mentor of mine is fond of saying. This kind of relationship grows your character over your ego. These types of people are not sycophantic suck-ups who tell you that you walk on water and who always and forever say yes. In fact, you can judge the health of a relationship based on one's ability to say no to the other. Surround yourself with good souls who can tell you no as easily as they tell you yes. This is yet another piece of advice from another mentor.

Relationships are often difficult to navigate on their own, but when they come through your calling or vocation, they bring a new dimension of complexity. Business engagements, contractual obligation, money, reputation, expectations, and communication style can all put an added strain on the relationship. Learning to navigate the labyrinth of professional relationships requires no small degree of discernment and grace. Establishing boundaries and concise communication practices is paramount. Inevitably, much of what you learn on this score will unfortunately come through trial and error. Relationships go sideways, opinions differ, tempers flare, feelings get hurt. Convention snags on the nail of conflict, and at once the nakedness of our humanity is revealed. The fortunate thing is that you are more likely to learn your lesson when it comes through the sting of real-world experience.

SURROUND YOURSELF WITH GOOD SOULS WHO CAN TELL YOU NO AS EASILY AS THEY TELL YOU YES.

The maker's heart can find its way to the relational richness by knowing where and how to dig.

Prospecting

A practice of gold miners is to pan a sample of dirt from a prospective plot of land before they bring in the big equipment and dig deep. If that pan yields a promising amount of flakes or even a couple of nuggets, then they will set up camp and bring in the big diggers and sluice box. But if there is no color in the pan, as they say, the miners will move on to new territory and try again somewhere else.

I think a similar approach to relationships is wise. Begin slow. Sift the topsoil of each other's personalities before you mine the bedrock of the other person's character. If there is potential for collaboration, it will pan out. If not, you won't have broken your back removing loads of relational overburden only to find yourself in a hole. I have been there, and believe me, it is not fun. If you want to get out of the hole, put down the shovel.

Beware the quick and dirty. There are some who like to rush relationship. Their cut-to-the-chase mentality may seem refreshingly honest at first, especially against the backdrop of other surface-level niceties that typically mark early acquaintances. These are the ones who ask you to divulge your deepest, darkest secrets after just learning your name. At first blush, they are more apt to perform an emotional Heimlich on you than shake your hand. As quickly as they barge in, they are prone to bolt. A forceful haste to natural, progressive familiarity is a sign of emotional unhealth and immaturity. Dump your pan and head for new ground.

Slowness in relationships, as in art, yields lasting value. Time

> SLOWNESS IN RELATIONSHIPS, AS IN ART, YIELDS LASTING VALUE.

is the greatest validation of trust. Those early stages of the relationship provide the opportunity to build a foundation of trust while still maintaining healthy boundaries. A dear friend of mine calls this *front porching.* Get to know someone on the outskirts of intimacy before you invite them across the threshold of friendship. People will actually respect you more if you take a measured approach to getting acquainted before jumping in with both feet.

Even God, who discerns our hearts, says, If I can trust you with a little, I can trust you with a lot (Luke 16:10). Though He is divine, He is modeling for us healthy relationships on our terms.

Let me take a moment to remind you exactly what we are looking for. I am not speaking of a mercenary relationship where money is its chief end. Yes, money is important, and I have covered that in the previous chapter, but what I am encouraging you toward is of greater and more lasting value. A relationship such as this, for all parties involved, transcends the transactional to become transformational. It does indeed happen at the level of the maker's heart.

Patrons

Patronage has a long and complicated history. Because my interests gravitate back to the Italian Renaissance, that period has shaped much of my thinking on the matter. During this time patronage was in large part the reason that the Renaissance happened at all. The unique relationship between patrons and makers proved to be a powerful combination, but not without complications. Politics, bureaucracy, family factions, warring states, and commerce often convoluted the creation process for the makers under the patron's employ.

I have had several patrons over the course of my career. I can boast a much healthier relationship with my patrons than most of the artists working during the Renaissance, and it all comes down to spiritual alignment. My patrons have supported me because they believed in the gift that God has given me. They have never once tried to get me to relinquish creative control or manipulate my abilities by their financial power. I have had only good souls come around me to call my gift to an even greater level.

I have had some who are patrons of the *person* (namely, me), investing in my infrastructure and enterprise, and patrons of the *piece*, meaning they are funding the creation of an art piece, the delivery of which marks the end of our collaborative engagement. The truth of the matter is, I might not have endeavored to do half of my greatest works or even become an artist full-time had it not been for the support of my patrons.

Makers need the support of patrons, even in our modern day. There is a kind of symbiosis that is achieved between the two that unleashes the capabilities of both for the good of culture. Makers bring a high level of specialized skill, vision, and passion, while patrons provide the means by which the maker is unleashed and their skill called to its highest level. Moreover, patrons, having great wealth and financial savvy, are gifted with a keen ability to unlock value wherever they see it—even in the heart of the maker!

As John Ruskin wrote in *A Joy for Ever*, "You have always to find your artist, not to make him; you can't manufacture him any more than you can manufacture gold. You can find him and refine him: you dig him out as he lies nugget-fashioned in the mountain-stream; you bring him home; and you make him into a current coin, or household plate, but not one grain of him can you originally produce."[1]

My patrons found me that way—*nugget-fashioned in the mountain-stream*. I was living at home with my parents after college. I was barely making ends meet while working on any art commission thrown my way, no matter how small. My very first patron, before he had become so, came to visit me at my parents' house to see what I was working on. I still remember that feeling of utter embarrassment as I gave him the "tour" of my corner studio in the basement. I thought he would see my underwhelming setup and run the other way. Surely he could see no promise there. But something glinted in his eye that day as he saw the promise of my makeup. He took a great risk to make something useful of me.

Kinfolk

I was an orphan artist. After being rejected from the art program at my alma mater (a story I tell at length in my previous book), I was wandering the landscape without a creative home to call my own. But in the summer of 2006 I ventured cross-country on a road trip with my dear mom to the exotic metropolis of Kansas City. There, in a moderately sized hotel, were gathered less than one hundred people for the annual penmen's conference. You might have never heard of a penman or that they have been known to conference, but so they do . . . annually. Only a few months prior had I learned both of these things for myself. And so it was at the ripe age of twenty-two that I made a pilgrimage to a city I had never been to, to meet a people I didn't know, to learn a craft that was all but dead.

After checking in at the front desk, I made my way to the small hotel ballroom, drawn there by a voice speaking on the overhead system, which I know so well now but was completely strange to me then. Through a crack in the double doors, I could finally see the speaker; it was Master Penman Michael Sull. Standing at a simple podium, he addressed the attendees gathered around circular tables throughout the room.

I wedged the door open and slid in sideways, quietly as I could, my mom close behind. I will never be able to recall what Michael said that evening, but I will never forget what I felt. My heart was pounding but for a reason I could not quite pin down. In hindsight, I can see the monumental twist of fate I was stepping into, but I didn't know that then—or perhaps I did. When Michael finished speaking, the crowd dispersed in a growing jovial chatter. As I looked about the room smiling, I locked eyes with a few strangers who reciprocated my gleam but with a quizzical slant. A few odd looks like this in quick succession made me feel as though I had crashed in on a family reunion, and so it was. But I was not made to feel strange; I was simply a stranger to them. And in a weird way this was a kind of comfort. In a group of people so familiar with one another, an outsider is quickly noticed, which gave me immediate insight into the comradely nature of the clan. And I was not a stranger long. Outstretched hands and hearty hellos clamored to me. Being so young in an otherwise *mature* gathering, one sweet lady asked, "Young man, are you lost?" I responded with a chuckle. "No, ma'am . . . I think I am found. I'm here for the penmen's conference."

It is rare in life to meet in one brief moment so many people who will mean so much to you for so long into the future. But so it was that evening. When I was finally introduced to Michael Sull, he shook my hand, looked me squarely in the eyes, and said, "Jake, it is a pleasure to meet you. I expect big things from you." Even as I write this, his words still make me tear up.

The whole week went on like that. I met Master Penman John DeCollibus for the first time—the very man who inspired me to pick up the pen through a video of him writing on YouTube. He was larger than life. Six foot three with nineteen-inch biceps. We sat down at lunch together that day and talked back and forth about the golden age of handwriting and the golden age of bodybuilding and our favorite characters from both. When John looked over my small portfolio of calligraphy, he said in his thick Bostonian accent, "Jake, this is too good. I'm sorry, but I'm gonna have to break your arms."

I met Neil McCaffery, who is the keeper of the archives. Neil faithfully retrieves the vast penmanship collection from a salt mine storage facility in Kansas each year and drives it literally anywhere in the country for the conference. In a designated suite in the hotel, Neil lays out the framed works and literal family albums full of world-class calligraphy. A quiet soul is Neil, and he walked me through album after album and page after page, introducing me to our forefathers of penmanship and the vast family tree I was being grafted into.

Late in the week my mom was sitting with the late, great Rick Muffler, who would later become my mentor through the Master Penman program. He told her that my coming there with all my passion had infused the group with new life. For years the gathering had languished with diminishing numbers and lack of interest in the craft. My coming was a glimmer of hope that there might be some out there to whom they could pass the baton.

Nearly twenty years on and the group boasts thousands of members worldwide. The conference is still held each year but is now quadruple what it was at when I first attended. Not for one second do I take credit for this resurgence; I was just the first wave of a rising tide.

My encouragement to you is to find a community like mine. Call them your tribe; call them your people. As for me, I call them family.

CHAPTER FIFTEEN

DETRACTORS

Defeating the Naysayers

I think this shall be a shorter chapter, for that is all detractors deserve. The one thing I can say about all of them from the get-go is they are not worth the time they are usually given.

The Critic

I have met a few art critics in person over the years, and whenever I reveal to them that I am an artist, I always get a similar reaction.

You would think they would be thrilled to meet someone who exists in their field of study and would relish the opportunity to hear from the horse's mouth about an artist's theory and approach. But you may be surprised, as I have been, to learn that their initial reaction is not so amicable. I would analogize it to a paleontologist coming face-to-face with a live dinosaur. Outside of the immediate fear of being eaten alive, there is yet another dread awakened in them at that moment, and this is the dread I see. There stands before them in flesh and blood one who can, in an instant, obliterate all their theories and scholarly wisdom merely by existing. An ounce of experience outweighs a truckload of opinion every time.

For this reason, I think such critics prefer that their specimens of study be preserved at a distance in the sands of history or obscurity, where they can more easily pick apart their petrified bones. Not all the opinions held by critics are negative, I might add, or even wrong, but there is something in their title that predisposes them to a kind of hierarchal mentality. I can certainly make allowances for the more fair-minded commentator who can issue praise as well as punishment, but the run-of-the-mill takedown artist should be met with a good deal of skepticism. And thus the critic becomes the criticized. They appear to think their gift to the world is to destroy the gifts of others. They are supposed to be "in the know," and finding fault where no one else can is their way of proving it, which additionally provides to them some level of job security.

I once attended a gathering of makers and heard a critic give a presentation on a recently deceased artist. He prefaced his talk with, "Look, I do not want to be a takedown artist," but then proceeded over the following hour to tear apart this poor creator in a scathing analysis of the artist's style, business practice, life, and character.

I generally take issue with those who preemptively try to excuse themselves from the sins they are about to commit. It is like the busybody who says, "I am not being a gossip, but let me tell you about what I just heard in confidence about so and so." A disclaimer on the sin does not absolve the sinner; it only condemns them all the more.

While I was not particularly a fan of the artist in question, having observed the critic lock him in stocks in the public square that day as a victim of his ridicule, I walked away from the humiliating experience with pity in my heart for that maker. I am not saying that all the critic had to say was unfounded. Anyone could see the downfalls in this artist's life, but the critic was the only one who made a PowerPoint presentation of them.

And here is where I really take issue. The artist was, in the end, an accomplished and prolific oil painter. He was an irrefutable master in his genre. And to my knowledge, the critic had never made a single painting in his entire life.

When I was a kid, I would occasionally go golfing with my dad and brother at the small course right across the street from our neighborhood. My dad taught me an important lesson while teeing off one day: "Don't laugh until you swing." I had gotten in the habit of heckling my brother in good fun. But my dad would always throw out this phrase as if it was one to live by. While I had some talent for the game in my youth, as I have grown, I have become a terrible golfer. After hacking my way around enough golf courses, I have given it up completely. When my dad, brother, and now brother-in-law invite me out for a round of golf, I tell them I will meet them afterward at the clubhouse for a cold one. They might tell me how terribly one of them played that day, but I never laugh, for I have not swung and golf is no longer my game.

I might be able to respect an art critic if they were an accomplished artist. But rarely have I found accomplished artists being critical of another's work. By and large, the great artists I know are not interested in tearing apart those they deem lesser artists; instead, they point out and praise the good ones they admire. They would much rather talk in positive terms than negative ones.

One of the greatest commentaries on the role of the critic comes from my favorite Pixar film, *Ratatouille.* The main antagonist in the film, a famed food critic named Anton Ego, says, "In many ways, the work of the critic is easy. We risk very little, yet enjoy a position over those who offer up their work and their selves to our judgment. We thrive on negative criticism, which is fun to write and to read. But the bitter truth we critics must face, the average piece of junk is probably more meaningful than our criticism designating it so."[1]

Fighting the Trolls

It is easier than ever to be a troll in the world of social media with its many dark places to skulk and hide. I have been fortunate to suffer the wrath of internet trolls only occasionally, but I have been bludgeoned a time or two with their knobby clubs of maliciousness and ire. From what little I care to know about the lifestyle and habits of trolls, they seem to feed on a heavy diet of envy. They cook it up in a boiling black pot of anger and season it heavily with bitterness over an open fire, fueled by the last homely house they destroyed. Such unsettling foods make them bluster and bloat, and their whole body is inflamed like a bad case of gout. Thus fueled, they slink from the shadows to go on their rampage.

Years ago, I was regularly harassed by a young woman who created many fake profiles on Instagram from which she would criticize my work. On her own profile she played the sweet and innocent young artist, but at night she would go a-trolling. Her sin eventually found her out, as it always does. She was doing the same thing to many other artists, and her unmasking was finally at hand when we all compared notes. I ended up blocking her and all her pseudonyms. For all I know, she is still lurking under a bridge somewhere.

More recently, my Instagram profile was hacked by some ponce in Turkey who went by the name of LAMBY. I am not sure how he came by the name, but judging by his poor English in his threatening emails, I'd wager it was perhaps the result of some bad translation work. LAMBY hardly strikes fear into the hearts of his victims. Poor little LAMBY must have been down on his luck because he was demanding that I pay him eight hundred dollars to regain access to my Instagram profile. Through a friend of a friend who worked at Facebook, we were able to regain control of my profile, and that wolf in sheep's clothing was banished into the dark forest of the internet from whence he came with his tail tucked between his legs.

As a standing policy, Hannah and I give trolls no quarter. The moment we receive any unwarranted negativity, we block them out. They don't deserve better than that, and we have more important things to do than mop up after some troll drags their nastiness through our house.

I have the added level of protection in the form of my fearsome wife. I do not actually run any of our social media profiles myself—Hannah does. About five years ago, Hannah took over everything, and it gave me a new lease on life. I have never looked back! I do not even have the apps on my phone, and I cannot tell you what a blessing that has been. I read comments, answer questions, and respond to DMs but always on her phone in limited amounts. She filters everything herself first. If there is an off-color comment, she deletes it and blocks the user. She has zero tolerance for nonsense, and I love that about her. She might describe the interchange to me, but if I ask to see it, well, it is too late. That ill-meaning sleuth has already been banished by Hannah back into the obscurity of the internet.

I think everyone should have their own version of a Hannah. She not only is amazing at creating content and enjoys doing it but also is not attached to my work in the same way I am. If someone lobs a fiery nastygram, she is quick to snuff it out. And given the fact that the vast, *vast* amount of comments we get are positive, she also protects me from getting a big head, as she says. Since I do not have direct access all the time, I cannot constantly check my profile and read the comments or track my engagement. As her husband, I am ever the guardian of her heart, but in this capacity, she is the guardian of mine.

Kings and Obscure Men

Several years ago, as my work was really taking off, a friend of ours at church shared with us a verse: "Do you see a man skillful in his work? He will stand before kings; he will not stand before obscure men" (Proverbs 22:29).

Within a few short weeks, two more people randomly shared this same verse with us—there God was again, speaking to me in threes! We have rehearsed this Scripture like a mantra ever since we learned of it. It has guided us through so many awkward encounters and relationships and also affirmed so many of the good ones. The nature of my work has raised me up before kings and obscure men alike. It has required a great deal of discernment and fortitude to identify the obscure ones we run into and shut them out the best we can. Obscure is the perfect way to describe the internet bullies who come looking for their pound of flesh.

Online interchanges do not afford you the same level of social accountability that an in-person interaction would. People often say things through their keyboard that would get them punched in the face if they said it in person. And so behind their keyboards they hide. These are precisely the types we avoid, and we will not stand before them.

Conversely, I have stood before kings. Men and women of great wealth, accomplishment, and character have sought me out. My art has taken me into realms I could have only dreamed of. I regularly turn to Hannah on such occasions and remark, "How in the world did we get here?!" Ironically and thankfully, the people I have stood before who actually do have the power and means to do me harm or abuse me never do. I am treated with such honor in their presence and probably more than I deserve. There is still a great deal of discernment required in these relationships as well, but thus far I have been deeply blessed at the hands of kings. That one little verse out of Proverbs paints a picture of my life.

I long for and encourage the same in your own life, dear reader. Don't give the internet sleuths any of your time or attention. Such obscure men strive only to do you harm. They are not worth reasoning with because they are unreasonable. They are not worth arguing with because arguing is their chief end. Envy and slander fuel their rage. In the end, it is not about you or what you create; it is entirely about them and their own insecurities. Better to knock the dust from your sandals and walk on.

The critic, likewise, should have little if any standing in your life. There might be the occasional fair-minded ones who may offer praise as well as criticism. They might give greater insight into your work or someone else's. I can accept substantiated historical facts from a critic, but when they shift into pure opinion, I take everything they say with a giant grain of salt. They are not the man in the arena. They risk no skin in the game.

> THE CONDITION OF YOUR MAKER'S HEART IS INFLUENCED GREATLY BY THE COMPANY YOU KEEP.

The condition of your maker's heart is influenced greatly by the company you keep. Find your kings of character; stand before the ones who want to champion you and your work. The detractors are not worth your time.

CHAPTER SIXTEEN

FINISHING WELL

The Last Battle

Art is never finished, only abandoned.

— Attributed to LEONARDO DA VINCI

If there is one thing harder than beginning an art piece, it is completing it. After tens, hundreds, or thousands of hours on a single work, at what *moment* can you finally declare, "It is finished"? There is always one more thing to do, one more detail to add, or one more feature to refine. After being depleted of all creative energy over the course of some grand creation, your final sprint to the finish is an uphill one. And instead of a definitive ribbon to run through or a chalked line to cross, the end of your maker's marathon is often ill-defined and anticlimactic.

Half of this battle is a mental one. After striving so long in "creator mode" and always approaching the project in that capacity, it is hard to see your creation as anything but a work in progress. Your unique relationship to what you make as its maker means that you will always frame it in your mind that way. Think of a parent who has a hard time letting go of their child as they reach adulthood. No matter how old they get, in the eyes of the parents, that son or daughter will always be their baby. This analogy might be a bit overwrought, but it points to the mental and emotional hurdle of relinquishing control of your creative offspring and letting it endure apart from you. Finishing well means learning to let go at the appropriate time.

THE END OF YOUR MAKER'S MARATHON IS OFTEN ILL-DEFINED AND ANTICLIMACTIC.

The other half of the battle comes in the form of the final push. A task nearing its end always feels the longest. Perhaps with the terminus in sight the anticipation builds to a fever pitch. Maintaining focus and not rushing the end is the final battle. Yet another parent–child dynamic serves as a fitting analogy: I have heard many parents describe the strain on their relationship with their adult children right before they fly the nest. Tensions seem to rise as the departure of their child draws near with a kind of unspoken expectation: *Shouldn't you be gone already?* Admittedly, I have experienced both of the aforementioned parental attitudes toward various pieces I have created over the years. For some I am the clingy, sentimental parent straining to let go. And for others I am glad to see the back of them when they finally do leave my home. Regardless of how I feel, I am the father of all I make, and doing right by my creations is owed to them in the end.

A Dismal End

Think of a TV series that was great for several seasons, only to have the writers botch the ending. Think of a novel that has the reader engrossed all the way through, only for the story to fall flat on its face in the final chapter. It is obvious to anyone when the wind has gone out of the maker's sails at the final leg of their journey. Perhaps their joy for work wanes at the end and is subconsciously expressed in the way they draw it to a miserable close. The depressed and lazy maker betrays themselves and all their efforts up to that point when they skirt their efforts at the final charge.

The thing that ties my hands to the mast at the final turn is the thought of my cumulative effort up to that point. Finishing well means ending with the same fervor I began with. More than that, I think how I am and *should be* a better creator than when I first started. The last push is my chance to prove it. I hunker down; I put the mental blinders on and comb over the piece in a final pass. I often make myself a punch list of final to-dos so that when I get all the way through it, I know the job is really and truly done.

FINISHING WELL MEANS ENDING WITH THE SAME FERVOR I BEGAN WITH.

Moreover, I strive to end with joy. I would not want my feelings over the entire piece to be soured by begrudging it at the finish. As I come to the final turn, I have every reason to celebrate and be happy. I think of all the cumulative enjoyment the piece has brought me up to that point and how I get to savor it one last time. I think of the pains and hurdles I worked through to bring it to its terminus and how they are not a worry anymore. Cheerfulness should fill my maker's heart when at length I see my full creation manifested before me. Sometimes this comes naturally, and other times I have to make a conscious decision to rejoice in my labor. Either way, my work should shine with a final varnish of my own incandescent joy.

Ceremony

As the end of an art piece is so nebulous, I take steps to make it feel more definitive. If it is a two-dimensional art piece, I take it on a ceremonial trip to the framers, getting it beautifully matted and framed. Once behind glass where I can no longer fiddle with it helps bring a sense of closure to the process. Going out with my wife for a beautiful celebratory dinner after the long haul of a major art piece ties a beautiful bow around the whole endeavor. Celebration is a very important part of the creative process. As God repeatedly did over the course of creation in Genesis, He looked on what He had made and called it good. Part of the *goodness* of what was made was the completeness of its making. In God's own way He was celebrating completion at every stage and at the end too. As imitators of God, with His Maker's heart reflected in ours, we should also take our cues from the good Lord on this point as well.

CELEBRATION IS A VERY IMPORTANT PART OF THE CREATIVE PROCESS.

Finishing *This* Well

Here am I at yet another grand conclusion while writing about finishing well. Every creation is a gift from God and an opportunity to joyously make. This book has been a gift and a challenge to me in so many ways. Writing is still my newest medium and the one I feel least confident in. Yet I am not alone in this effort. A number of fellow makers have joined me in the formation of this book, and I am grateful for each and every one of them. I know they help fill in where I lack.

Having the opportunity to write in depth and at length about the creative process was a tremendous gift to me. Part of my mission and calling as an artist is helping others learn how to create with greater effectiveness, efficiency, and intimacy with God.

It has not only honed my ability to communicate to you, my fellow makers, but it has also given me the chance to deeply analyze my approach. In words commonly attributed to the Nobel Prize–winning physicist Richard Feynman, "If you want to master something, teach it." Synthesizing so much of what I have learned over my career as an artist here within these pages has allowed me to take account of what I know. I have been able to reflect on where I stumbled across those golden nuggets of wisdom and collect them all here. Having not gone to art school in the first place, I am not merely repeating the nostrums of any singular institution. What I know was not cooked up in the sterile halls of academia but harvested from wild hills and dark valleys in the final frontier of experience. What wisdom I've borrowed is a hodgepodge of information gathered from fellow travelers along the way. Each tidbit of insight has proven its value and served me well the last decade and a half.

What you hold in your hand is the precious gem, neatly faceted and highly polished over many rounds of edits and design phases. The culmination of many different makers bringing their skills to bear. But it was retrieved from the deepest and darkest caverns of my life. Not once was I sequestered away on some ideal writer's retreat to compose my words in tranquil silence. Not once did the storms of life relent while I poured my heart out on my keyboard. My office door was my only available barrier against the torrent of everyday storms, which I could duck behind only occasionally.

My wife and children—God love them—permeated that thin shroud continuously. Most of this book I have written in the thin margins of life. It has been my war journal in the foxhole. I have jotted it down bit by bit in every scenario you can imagine. Between chisel strokes in the woodshop, I would blow the sawdust from my keyboard to whittle on a thought or carve out a story. On the way to visit my in-laws in Wyoming, I sat in the passenger seat of our Toyota Highlander, packed with luggage and kids, navigating the traffic of my thoughts on my laptop. While our son and the neighbor boy were at tae kwon do practice every Tuesday, I sat beside the other parents in a cluster of folding chairs at the far corner of the dojang, striking the keyboard to the sounds of *ki-hup*s and punching bag blows.

And even here at the final turn of these pages, the battles do not relent. There is yet one more story that seems almost too obvious not to include on this final day of writing this book. We currently have a house painter repainting the exterior of the house. It, too, is his last day on the project. He called to me earlier to let me know that a rattlesnake had burrowed itself in a hole at the base of our foundation. That hole happens to be right underneath my studio where I am writing. Trying to return to my manuscript but knowing the snake was there made me feel as if he was coiled under my chair and ready to strike. Try as I might to concentrate, I could not settle my nerves till I knew the invading serpent was vanquished.

Living near the foothills of the Rockies, we see our share of wildlife, but the rattlesnake has always been the one that fills me with the most dread for the safety of my young children, who play constantly outside and rarely in shoes. I invested in a pair of snake tongs some years ago to deal with such varmints. I have used them on a few bull snakes and garters, but this was the first rattler I've had to contend with in the seven-plus years of living here. So today of all days feels significant. I fetched the snake tongs from the shed.

Back inside my scriptorium, I popped the screen out of my corner window, which gave me a peephole of my own to poke out of, and looked directly down on the mouth of the snake's lair. Despite the vileness of the creature and the looming danger, I thought of how comical the scene must have looked from the outside. *Jake versus snake*, popping our heads out of our respective holes and in turn pulling them back in again.

Finally, the draw of the morning sun coaxed that cold-blooded schemer fully out of his hole, and he gathered some two feet of length in a lazy coil against the foundation of the house. My chance had arrived! I put on my cowboy boots and grabbed the snake tongs, which were leaning against the corner of the room like some homesteader's ready shotgun. I walked around the corner of the house and made my quiet approach to that sun-basking belly-slider. With tongs at the ready and my arm cocked back, this scaly demon would get a taste of his own medicine and learn for the first and last time what it is like to be struck. And strike I did! With the jaws of the tongs wide open, I jabbed at the thickest tangle of coils and clamped down hard on the scissor-grip. Immediately, his rattle shook with fury. With quick successive strikes, he bit at the tongs in venomous anger. I carried his scaly, writhing body to a dry patch of dirt and grabbed a spade shovel. For all his long-bodied, long-fanged, long-rattling fight, I cut him down to size. I buried his head in the dirt, stomped the ground with my boot, and got back to the business of finishing my book. My casual return to work was as if to say to that vanquished viper, "You might be the last interruption I've had to contend with while writing this book, but you are hardly the scariest."

I have long discovered from the start of this manuscript that I must fight *and* write. My lesson lived is yours learned, and that is my gift to you. Do not give up the fight! But also do not give up creating while you are fighting, for that is your fight as well. I know that is a lot to ask, believe me! There is really no other way. Even when there is a serpent lurking at your window, crush its head and get right back to work. What you are creating is too important not to finish and finish well!

DO NOT GIVE UP CREATING WHILE YOU ARE FIGHTING.

Like that story of me in the cave as a boy in chapter 1, every word of this was squeezed out of me in the narrow passages of my humble, everyday existence. With my elbows dug deep in the mud and the weight of a mountain on my back, my maker's heart was thus compressed. Beneath such forces it was not hardened but crystallized, and not to stone but diamond made. And this I find to be the forging process of every maker's heart: The heat of creation compounds with the pressures of life over the slow crawl of time to transform the very core of you into something that better holds the light.

When at length you have reached the deepest recesses of life in caverns deep or cathedrals old, the flame that shines is not the torch in your hand but the maker's heart in your chest, burning brighter than a thousand candles with the eternal glow of the light of Christ.

ACKNOWLEDGMENTS

MY AMAZING WIFE, HANNAH

As E. E. Cummings said, "I carry your heart with me (I carry it in my heart)."[1] So, while it is my maker's heart within these pages, yours is here too. It is here in the ways you have uplifted and cared for mine; it is here in our shared passions; it is here in my courage, for you have made me brave; it is here in my boldness, for you have made me strong; it is here in my tenderness, for you have made me meek; and it is here in my prudence, for you have made me wise. For all that and more, I love you!

LISA-JO BAKER

If not for you, I might never have written a book at all. Yours was the hand that pulled me down the rabbit's hole of the literary world with its many scary unknowns and magical discoveries. Patiently you waited till I finished my first book before we worked cooperatively on this one. You were with me in the cave through blinding darkness and narrow passages, and you always helped me find the light. More than an editor, I shall always call you friend!

MOM AND DAD

While my life and character have ever been shaped by you, this book marks a season during which I leaned on you greatly. Thank you so much for the parents and grandparents you are and for your willingness to always lend a hand or send a prayer. I love you both so much!

STEVE AND ELAINE MUSIC

You have always said my best work is still in me. Thank you for believing that when I could not believe it for myself. You've seen me through nearly fifteen years of working as an artist and have helped me do the work God has called me to. Thank you for holding my hand to the plow. This book holds many of the stories we lived together.

JENNI BURKE

Thank you for always being such a genuine encouragement to me throughout this process. Hannah and I thank the Lord for you regularly and cannot imagine navigating the literary world without you. Beyond that, you have been a dear friend and tender to the struggles we faced while writing this book. We know what the Enemy intended for evil, God will use for good. And He already has.

NOTES

CHAPTER 1: ENTERING IN: Caves and Cathedrals

1. G. K. Chesterton, *The Everlasting Man* (Hodder and Stoughton, 1925), 32.
2. C. S. Lewis, *Surprised by Joy* (HarperOne, 2017), 206.

CHAPTER 2: PRACTICE: Progress over Perfection

1. Andrew Murray, *Humility: The Beauty of Holiness* (Anson D.F. Randolph & Co, 1985), 62, https://hdl.handle.net/2027/nnc1.cr60039221.

CHAPTER 3: INSPIRATION: Striking a Spark in a Hurricane

1. C. S. Lewis, *The Four Loves* (Harcourt Inc., 1960).
2. Maxi Heitmayer and Saadi Lahlou, "Why Are Smartphones Disruptive? An Empirical Study of Smartphone Use in Real-Life Contexts," *Computers in Human Behavior* 116, no. 106637 (2021), https://doi.org/10.1016/j.chb.2020.106637.

CHAPTER 4: IDEATION: From Musing to Making

1. W. B. Yeats, "He Wishes for the Cloth of Heaven," The Poetry Society, accessed December 10, 2025, https://poetrysociety.org.uk/poems/he-wishes-for-the-cloth-of-heaven-2/.
2. G. K. Chesterton, *Orthodoxy* (Hendrickson, 2006), 28.
3. Jane Austen, *Pride and Prejudice* (Doubleday, 1945), 190.

CHAPTER 5: THE SKETCH: Start Small

1. C. S. Lewis, *On Writing (and Writers)* (HarperCollins, 2022), 38.

CHAPTER 8: UNDERPAINTING: The Unseen Work

1. J. R. R. Tolkien, *The Fellowship of The Ring* (Houghton Mifflin Harcourt, 1954), 77.

CHAPTER 10: PENTIMENTO: True Repentance

1. Merriam-Webster, s.v. "ASMR," accessed April 30, 2026, https://www.merriam-webster.com/dictionary/asmr.
2. *The Agony and the Ecstasy*, directed by Carol Reed (20th Century Fox, 1965), film.

CHAPTER 11: THE ART OF SLOW: Making Work that Lasts

1. J. R. R. Tolkien, *The Two Towers* (Houghton Mifflin Harcourt, 1954), 454.
2. John Ruskin, *A Joy for Ever* (George Allen & Sons, Ruskin House, 1911), 47.

CHAPTER 12: PRAY YOUR WORK: Laying Your Heart on the Page

1. C. S. Lewis, *The Problem of Pain* (HarperOne, 1996), 91.

CHAPTER 13: FEAST AND FAMINE: Finding Financial Stability

1. Jacques Maritain, *The Responsibility of the Artist* (Gordian Press, 1972), 44.

CHAPTER 14: SUPPORTERS: The Art of Relationship

1. Ruskin, *A Joy for Ever*, 34.

CHAPTER 15: DETRACTORS: Defeating the Naysayers

1. *Ratatouille*, directed by Brad Bird (Pixar Animation Studios, 2007), film.

ACKNOWLEDGMENTS

1. E. E. Cummings, "i carry your heart with me [i carry it in]," Poetry Foundation, accessed May 2, 2026, https://www.poetryfoundation.org/poetrymagazine/poems/49493/i-carry-your-heart-with-mei-carry-it-in.

ABOUT THE AUTHOR

Jake Weidmann is a professional artist and certified as one of nine Master Penmen in the world. Certified through IAMPETH (International Association of Master Penmen, Engrossers and Teachers of Handwriting) in July 2011, Weidmann holds the title as the youngest Master Penman by three decades and the youngest to ever attain the title. His journey into calligraphy has been the "special sauce" for everything he now creates, as he incorporates traditional calligraphic flourishing into his fine art. Weidmann is self-taught in each of his disciplines (calligraphy, painting, drawing, woodworking, sculpting, engraving, and jewelry design). Weidmann's analog mediums defy our digital-centric age as he employs old-world tools and techniques to achieve his finished works. Following the disciplines of past masters, he is resurrecting ancient artforms by working with both private patrons and corporate clients. He lives and works with his wife, Hannah, raising their four children in the foothills of Colorado.

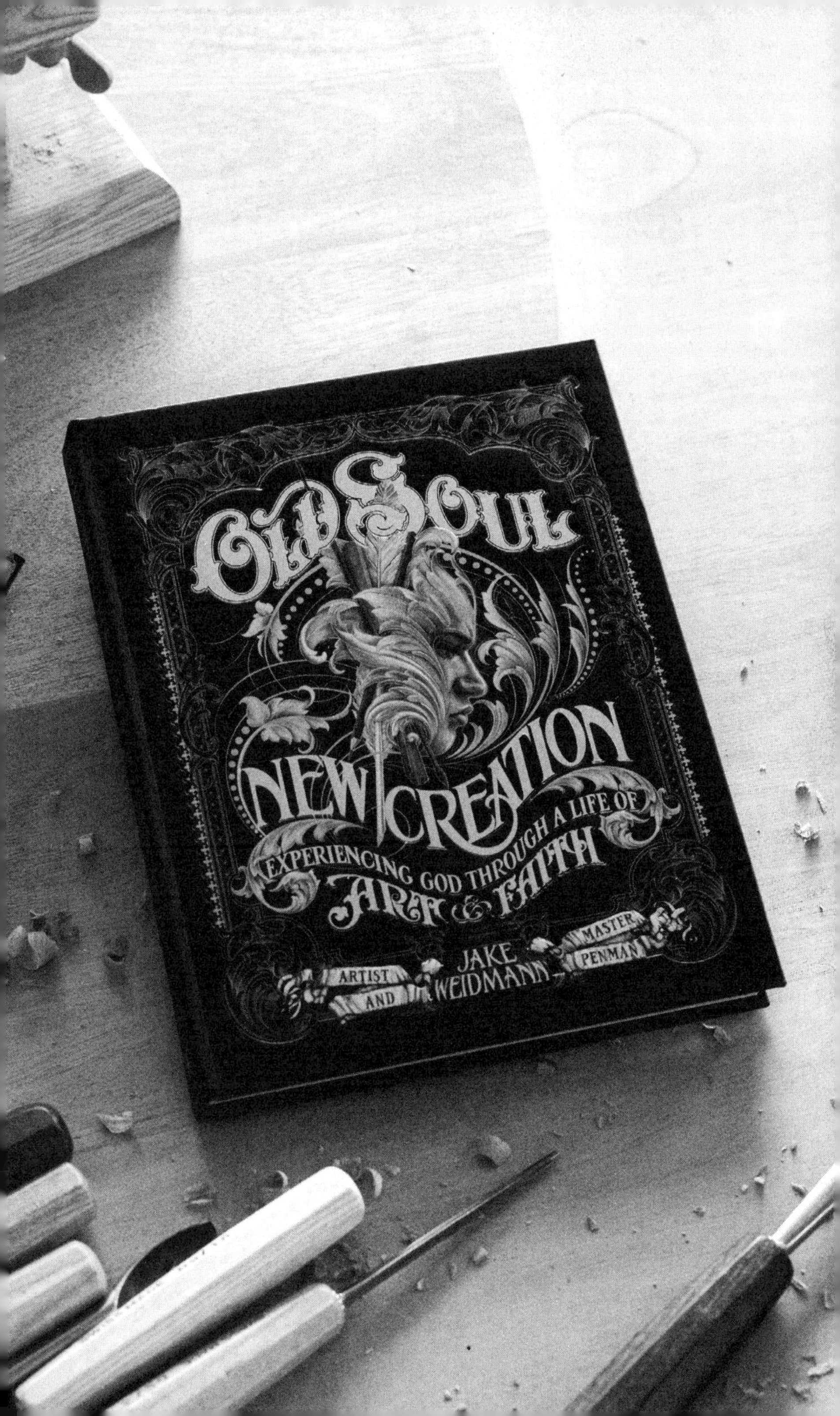

OLD SOUL
NEW CREATION
EXPERIENCING GOD THROUGH A LIFE OF
ART & FAITH
ARTIST AND MASTER PENMAN
JAKE WEIDMANN

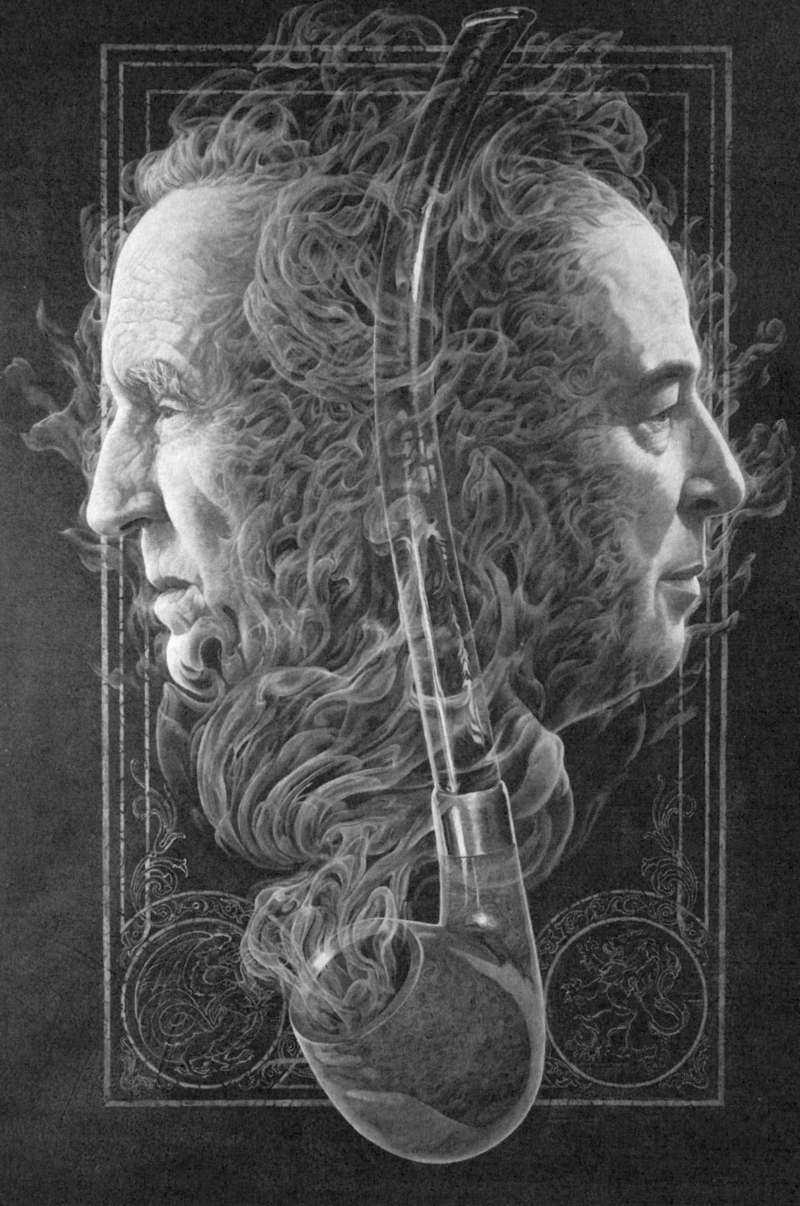

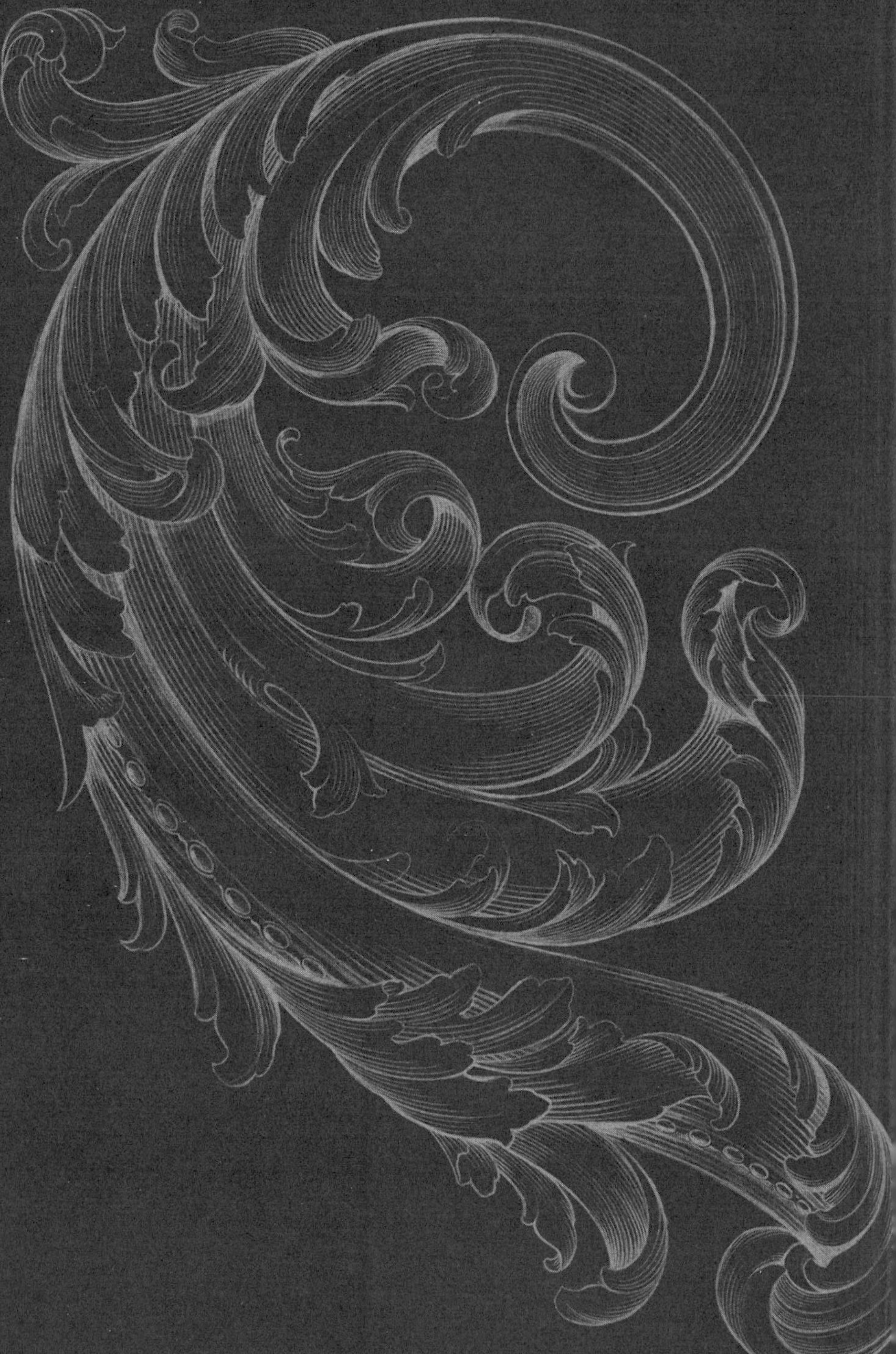